EASY FRENCH SHORT STORIES For Beginners

Learn to Speak French Quickly with the FluentBridge Translation Method

www.fluentbridgepublishing.com

ISBN: 978-1-0690720-0-9

www.fluentbridgepublishing.com

Learning a new language can feel overwhelming. We understand how frustrating it is to read a text and struggle to understand it, or to learn vocabulary that you later forget.

The challenge isn't just reading; it is retaining vocabulary, understanding sentence structure, and being able to use what you have learned in real conversations.

That is why this book is more than just a collection of stories. It is a step-by-step learning experience designed to help you think in French while naturally improving your reading, comprehension, and speaking skills.

Using the FluentBridge Translation Method, you will not just see a translation, but understand exactly how French sentences are structured. This will make it easier to grasp grammar, expand your vocabulary, and apply what you learn.

With audio recordings, guided translations, and comprehension exercises, this book gives you the tools to grow your confidence in French, one story at a time.

Our Mission

At FluentBridge, our goal is to make learning a language practical, structured, and accessible. We believe that the best way to learn is through clear explanations, meaningful practice, and gradual exposure to French texts in a way that makes sense for beginners.

Your journey to mastering French starts here.
We truly hope you enjoy the process!

Welcome to Easy French Short Stories for Beginners!

This book is designed to guide you through learning French in a practical, engaging, and structured way. With carefully crafted stories, translations, comprehension questions, and an answer key, you'll develop your French skills step by step.

How Each Story is Structured

Every story is presented in four sections to make the learning process easy and enjoyable:

1. Short Story

- **Full French Immersion:** Each story is written entirely in French to help you immerse yourself in the language and develop natural comprehension skills.

- **Practical Themes:** The stories focus on everyday situations such as family, vacations, and daily routines, ensuring that you learn vocabulary you can use in real life.

- **Progressive Learning Approach:** Each story is designed to gradually build your learning by focusing on specific verb tenses and main persons (e.g., first-person singular, third-person plural). This structured progression allows you to internalize French grammar naturally, making it easier to apply in real conversations.

- **Listen to the Audio File:** Each story comes with an audio recording in three speeds:

    - Slow: for better clarity and easier understanding.

    - Normal: to train your ear for natural spoken French.

- Fast: to challenge your comprehension skills.

- **Pronunciation Practice:** Listen to the audio and repeat after each sentence to improve your pronunciation, intonation, and fluency.

2. Explore the Translation

This section uses the FluentBridge Translation Method, which breaks down each sentence into three parts:

- French Sentence (FS): The original French sentence.
- Literal Translation (LT): A word-for-word breakdown to show sentence structure.
- Natural Translation (NT): A smooth English translation for clear understanding.

Use this section to learn new vocabulary, understand grammar, and see how French sentences are constructed.

3. Put Your Learning to the Test

- After each story, you'll find a set of comprehension questions to test your understanding.
- These questions include sentence translations, true or false exercises, and sentence completions, helping you reinforce what you've learned.

4. Answer Key

Verify your answers using the answer key to track your progress and pinpoint areas for review.

How to Get the Most Out of This Book

1. Listen First: Start by listening to the audio file for each story to familiarize yourself with pronunciation and rhythm. Choose from slow, normal, or fast speeds depending on your comfort level.

2. Read the Story: Read through the story in French, even if you don't understand every word initially. Focus on recognizing familiar words and getting the overall meaning.

3. Listen & Repeat: Play the audio again and pause after each sentence to repeat it out loud. This will help improve your pronunciation, intonation, and fluency.

4. Explore the Translation: Use the FluentBridge Translation Method to break down each sentence and learn new words, phrases, grammar, and sentence structure.

5. Test Yourself: Complete the comprehension questions to solidify your understanding. You can do this on a sheet of paper, in a journal, or in our notebook companion, designed to help you stay organized and track your progress.

6. Review with the Answer Key: Use the answer key to check your answers, track your progress, and identify areas for improvement.

How Does It Work?

Each story in this book includes translations presented in a special format:

- **French Sentence (FS):** The original sentence in French.
- **Literal Translation (LT):** A word-for-word translation to help you understand the structure of the French sentence and how it differs from English.
- **Natural Translation (NT):** A smooth, natural English equivalent of the French sentence.

Note: When the literal and natural translations are identical, they are combined as LT/NT.

Example 1:

FS ▶ Je me regarde dans le miroir et je me brosse les dents.

LT ▶ I myself look in the mirror and I myself brush the teeth.

▼

NT ▶ I look at myself in the mirror and brush my teeth.

•••

Example 2:

FS ▶ Nous sommes une famille de quatre : mes parents, ma petite sœur et moi.

LT/NT ▶ We are a family of four: my parents, my little sister, and me.

•••

Note: The Natural Translation (NT) aims to provide the clearest and most commonly used way to express the sentence in English. However, there are often multiple valid ways to phrase a translation naturally. We've chosen the most intuitive option to help you understand the meaning without unnecessary complexity.

Why Is This Method Effective?

1. Understand French Grammar Instantly: By seeing how French sentences are constructed, you'll develop a better grasp of grammar without memorizing rules.

2. Expand Your Vocabulary Easily: Each story introduces practical, high-frequency words and phrases, helping you build a strong foundation in French.

3. Boost Your Confidence: The translations ensure you understand every sentence, allowing you to progress without frustration.

4. Engage with Audio: Each French story includes an audio recording to help you practice listening and understanding spoken French.

This method allows you to learn naturally, one step at a time, while enjoying engaging stories that gradually increase in complexity.

Claim Your Essential Free Bonus Downloads!

As a thank you for choosing Easy French Short Stories for Beginners, we've included exclusive learning resources to help you improve even faster!

Included Bonuses

- **Audio Files for Every Story** – Available in three speeds:

  - Slow: for better clarity and easier understanding.

  - Normal: to train your ear for natural spoken French.

  - Fast: to challenge your comprehension skills.

- **1000 Most Frequently Used French Words** – Expand your vocabulary with the most essential words for learning French.

- **Anki Flashcard Deck** – Memorize key vocabulary effortlessly with spaced repetition flashcards.

- **Extra Grammar Guide with Exercises and Solutions** – Strengthen your understanding with additional practice exercises and answer keys.

How to Access Your Bonuses

Scan the QR code below

or visit:

www.fluentbridgepublishing.com/efss-bonuses/

As you begin your journey with the Easy French Short Stories series, it's essential to have a space where you can jot down notes, track your progress, and organize what you've learned.

While you can use any paper or blank journal for this purpose, we've created the **FluentBridge Workbook Companion** to make your learning experience smoother, more effective, and help you monitor your improvement step by step.

Scan the QR code below to find it on Amazon.

What Is the FluentBridge Workbook Companion?

This specially designed workbook is tailored to accompany Easy French Short Stories (Volumes 1 and 2). It includes:

- **My Learning Goals:** Define your motivation, set clear objectives, and outline your language-learning journey.

- **My Progress Tracker:** Track your achievements as you complete each story and expand your vocabulary.

- **My Story Notes:** Write down key grammar points, reflections, and phrases for each story. This section also includes space to answer the comprehension exercises from the Put Your Learning to the Test section at the end of each story.

- **My Vocabulary Builder:** Create your own personalized dictionary of nouns, verbs, adjectives, and other words to reinforce your learning.

- **My Fun Word Search Challenge:** Strengthen your vocabulary with engaging word search puzzles based on the stories.

- **My Language Journal:** Practice writing in French by journaling your thoughts, progress, and newly learned phrases.

Why Choose the FluentBridge Workbook Companion?

While you can certainly use any notebook or journal, here's why the **FluentBridge Workbook Companion** is the ideal choice:

- **Structured for Learning:** Designed with dedicated sections for goal setting, progress tracking, story notes, vocabulary building, word search puzzles, and journaling—keeping everything organized in one place.

- **Active Learning for Better Retention:** Instead of just reading the stories, you engage with them through story notes, where you reflect on key grammar points, new vocabulary, and phrases. You can also answer the **Put Your Learning to the Test** exercises, helping you analyze and retain the material more effectively.

- **Custom-Fit to the Method:** Specifically created to complement the **FluentBridge Translation Method**, making learning and tracking progress seamless and intuitive.

- **Engaging and Interactive:** Includes **fun word search challenges** to reinforce vocabulary while keeping learning enjoyable.

- **Plenty of Space:** Generous room for recording new words, grammar tips, reflections, and personal insights without worrying about running out of pages.

- **A Keepsake of Your Journey:** As you complete the workbook, you'll have a tangible record of your progress—proof of how far you've come in your French-learning adventure!

Start Your Journey with the Right Tools

The FluentBridge Workbook Companion is available wherever this book is sold. It's an investment in your success and will help you stay organized, motivated, and on track.

Main verb tense:
Present simple
(Présent de l'indicatif)

Main person:
1st person singular
(1ère personne du singulier)

Text type:
First-person narrative
(Récit à la première personne)

Vocabulary theme:
Morning routine
(La routine matinale)

Listening to the story is key to mastering pronunciation and an essential step in your learning journey.

- Start with **slow audio** if you need extra clarity.
- Listen at **normal speed** to get used to natural French.
- Challenge yourself with **fast audio** when you're ready.
- **Practice pronunciation:** Pause after each sentence and repeat it out loud!

Find the audio download on page 12.

La routine matinale de Julie

Je m'appelle Julie. J'ai vingt-cinq ans et je vis à Paris. Chaque matin, ma journée commence de la même façon. Je veux vous raconter ma routine matinale.

À six heures et demie, mon réveil sonne. Je ne me lève pas tout de suite. Je reste dans mon lit pendant quelques minutes. J'aime ce moment de calme avant de commencer ma journée.

À six heures quarante-cinq, je sors enfin de mon lit. Je vais directement dans la salle de bain. Je me regarde dans le miroir et je me brosse les dents. Ensuite, je prends une douche rapide. L'eau chaude me réveille complètement.

Après ma douche, je retourne dans ma chambre pour m'habiller. Je choisis mes vêtements pour la journée. Aujourd'hui, je mets un jean bleu et un t-shirt blanc. Je me coiffe devant le miroir. Mes cheveux sont longs, alors je les attache en queue de cheval.

Il est maintenant sept heures et quart. Je vais dans la cuisine pour préparer mon petit-déjeuner. J'ouvre le réfrigérateur et je prends du lait et des fruits. Je mange toujours des céréales avec des fruits frais. C'est bon pour la santé ! Je bois aussi un grand verre de jus d'orange et un café.

Pendant que je mange, j'allume mon téléphone. Je regarde mes messages et je vérifie la météo pour la journée. Il fait beau aujourd'hui, le soleil brille dehors.

Après le petit-déjeuner, je retourne dans la salle de bain. Je me brosse à nouveau les dents et je me maquille légèrement. Je mets un peu de mascara et de rouge à lèvres.

Il est presque huit heures. Je prépare mon sac pour le travail. Je vérifie que j'ai tout ce dont j'ai besoin : mon ordinateur portable, mon téléphone, mes clés, et mon portefeuille.

Avant de partir, je fais le tour de mon appartement. Je ferme les fenêtres et j'éteins toutes les lumières. Je n'oublie pas de donner à manger à mon chat, Mina. Il miaule pour me dire au revoir.

À huit heures précises, je sors de chez moi. Je descends les escaliers de mon immeuble et je marche jusqu'à la station de métro. Le métro est toujours plein de monde le matin, mais j'aime observer les gens autour de moi.

Vingt minutes plus tard, j'arrive à mon bureau. Ma journée de travail peut commencer. Je suis prête à affronter cette nouvelle journée avec énergie et bonne humeur.

C'est ainsi que se déroule ma routine matinale. Elle est simple, mais elle me permet de bien commencer chaque jour.

Explore the Translation

FS ▶ La routine matinale de Julie

LT ▶ The routine morning of Julie

▼

NT ▶ Julie's morning routine

FS ▶ Je m'appelle Julie. J'ai vingt-cinq ans et je vis à Paris.

LT ▶ I myself call Julie. I have twenty-five years and I live at Paris.

▼

NT ▶ My name is Julie. I am twenty-five years old, and I live in Paris.

FS ▶ Chaque matin, ma journée commence de la même façon.

LT ▶ Each morning, my day begins of the same way.

▼

NT ▶ Every morning, my day starts the same way.

FS ▶ Je veux vous raconter ma routine matinale.

LT ▶ I want to you tell my routine morning.

NT ▶ I want to tell you about my morning routine.

•••

FS ▶ À six heures et demie, mon réveil sonne. Je ne me lève pas tout de suite.

LT ▶ At six hours and half, my alarm rings. I myself get up not right away.

▼

NT ▶ At six-thirty, my alarm rings. I don't get up right away.

•••

FS ▶ Je reste dans mon lit pendant quelques minutes.

LT ▶ I stay in my bed during some minutes.

▼

NT ▶ I stay in bed for a few minutes.

•••

FS ▶ J'aime ce moment de calme avant de commencer ma journée.

LT ▶ I like this moment of calm before of to begin my day.

▼

NT ▶ I enjoy this calm moment before starting my day.

•••

FS ▶ À six heures quarante-cinq, je sors enfin de mon lit.

LT ▶ At six hours forty-five, I go out finally from my bed.

▼

NT ▶ At six forty-five, I finally get out of bed.

•••

FS ▶ Je vais directement dans la salle de bain.

LT ▶ I go directly in the room of bath.

▼

NT ▶ I go straight to the bathroom.

•••

FS ▶ Je me regarde dans le miroir et je me brosse les dents.

LT ▶ I myself look in the mirror and I myself brush the teeth.

NT ▶ I look at myself in the mirror and brush my teeth.

•••

FS ▶ Ensuite, je prends une douche rapide.

LT ▶ Then, I take a shower quick.

NT ▶ Then, I take a quick shower.

•••

FS ▶ L'eau chaude me réveille complètement.

LT ▶ The water hot me wakes up completely.

NT ▶ The hot water fully wakes me up.

•••

FS ▶ Après ma douche, je retourne dans ma chambre pour m'habiller.

LT ▶ After my shower, I return in my room for myself to dress.

NT ▶ After my shower, I go back to my room to get dressed.

•••

FS ▶ Je choisis mes vêtements pour la journée.

LT ▶ I choose my clothes for the day.

▼

NT ▶ I choose my clothes for the day.

•••

FS ▶ Aujourd'hui, je mets un jean bleu et un t-shirt blanc.

LT ▶ Today, I put a jean blue and a t-shirt white.

NT ▶ Today, I'm wearing blue jeans and a white t-shirt.

•••

FS ▶ Je me coiffe devant le miroir.

LT ▶ I myself comb in front of the mirror.

▼

NT ▶ I do my hair in front of the mirror.

•••

FS ▶ Mes cheveux sont longs, alors je les attache en queue de cheval.

LT ▶ My hair is long, so I them tie in ponytail.

▼

NT ▶ My hair is long, so I tie it in a ponytail.

•••

FS ▶ Il est maintenant sept heures et quart.

LT ▶ It is now seven hours and quarter.

▼

NT ▶ It's now a quarter past seven.

•••

FS ▶ Je vais dans la cuisine pour préparer mon petit-déjeuner.

LT ▶ I go in the kitchen for to prepare my breakfast.

▼

NT ▶ I go to the kitchen to make my breakfast.

•••

FS ▶ J'ouvre le réfrigérateur et je prends du lait et des fruits.

LT ▶ I open the fridge and I take some milk and some fruits.

▼

NT ▶ I open the fridge and grab some milk and fruit.

•••

FS ▶ C'est bon pour la santé !

LT ▶ It is good for the health !

▼

NT ▶ It's healthy !

•••

FS ▶ Je mange toujours des céréales avec des fruits frais.

LT ▶ I eat always some cereals with some fruits fresh.

▼

NT ▶ I always eat cereal with fresh fruit.

•••

FS ▶ Je bois aussi un grand verre de jus d'orange et un café.

LT ▶ I drink also a big glass of juice of orange and a coffee.

NT ▶ I also drink a big glass of orange juice and a coffee.

•••

FS ▶ Pendant que je mange, j'allume mon téléphone.

LT ▶ While I eat, I turn on my phone.

▼

NT ▶ While I eat, I turn on my phone.

•••

FS ▶ Je regarde mes messages et je vérifie la météo pour la journée.

LT ▶ I look at my messages and I check the weather for the day.

▼

NT ▶ I check my messages and the weather for the day.

•••

FS ▶ Il fait beau aujourd'hui, le soleil brille dehors.

LT ▶ It makes nice today, the sun shines outside.

▼

NT ▶ It's nice out today; the sun is shining.

FS ▶ Après le petit-déjeuner, je retourne dans la salle de bain.
LT ▶ After the breakfast, I return in the room of bath.
▼
NT ▶ After breakfast, I go back to the bathroom.

FS ▶ Je me brosse à nouveau les dents et je me maquille légèrement.
LT ▶ I myself brush again the teeth and I myself put on makeup lightly.
▼
NT ▶ I brush my teeth again and put on a little makeup.

FS ▶ Je mets un peu de mascara et de rouge à lèvres.
LT ▶ I put a little of mascara and of lipstick.
▼
NT ▶ I put on a little mascara and lipstick.

FS ▶ Il est presque huit heures. Je prépare mon sac pour le travail.
LT ▶ It is almost eight hours. I prepare my bag for the work.
▼
NT ▶ It's almost eight o'clock. I get my bag ready for work.

FS ▶ Je vérifie que j'ai tout ce dont j'ai besoin : mon ordinateur portable, mon téléphone, mes clés, et mon portefeuille.
LT ▶ I check that I have all that which I have need : my laptop, my phone, my keys, and my wallet.
▼
NT ▶ I check that I have everything I need:my laptop, my phone, my keys, and my wallet.

FS ▶ Avant de partir, je fais le tour de mon appartement.

LT ▶ Before of to leave, I make the tour of my apartment.

NT ▶ Before leaving, I go around my apartment.

•••

FS ▶ Je ferme les fenêtres et j'éteins toutes les lumières.

LT ▶ I close the windows and I turn off all the lights.

NT ▶ I close the windows and turn off all the lights.

•••

FS ▶ Je n'oublie pas de donner à manger à mon chat, Mina.

LT ▶ I not forget to give to eat to my cat, Mina.

NT ▶ I don't forget to feed my cat, Mina.

•••

FS ▶ Il miaule pour me dire au revoir.

LT ▶ He meows for me to say goodbye.

NT ▶ He meows to say goodbye.

•••

FS ▶ À huit heures précises, je sors de chez moi.

LT ▶ At eight hours precise, I go out of my home.

NT ▶ At exactly eight o'clock, I leave home.

•••

FS ▶ Je descends les escaliers de mon immeuble et je marche jusqu'à la station de métro.

LT ▶ I go down the stairs of my building and I walk until the station of metro.

NT ▶ I go down the stairs of my building and walk to the metro station.

∙∙∙

FS ▶ Le métro est toujours plein de monde le matin, mais j'aime observer les gens autour de moi.

LT ▶ The metro is always full of people the morning, but I like to observe the people around of me.

NT ▶ The metro is always crowded in the morning, but I enjoy watching the people around me.

∙∙∙

FS ▶ Vingt minutes plus tard, j'arrive à mon bureau.

LT ▶ Twenty minutes more late, I arrive at my office.

NT▶ Twenty minutes later, I arrive at my office.

∙∙∙

FS ▶ Ma journée de travail peut commencer.

LT ▶ My day of work can begin.

NT ▶ My workday can begin.

∙∙∙

FS ▶ Je suis prête à affronter cette nouvelle journée avec énergie et bonne humeur.

LT ▶ I am ready to face this new day with energy and good mood.

NT ▶ I am ready to face the new day with energy and a good mood.

∙∙∙

FS ▶ C'est ainsi que se déroule ma routine matinale.

LT ▶ It is thus that itself unfolds my routine morning.

▼

NT ▶ This is how my morning routine goes.

•••

FS ▶ Elle est simple, mais elle me permet de bien commencer chaque jour.

LT ▶ It is simple, but it me allows of well to start each day.

▼

NT ▶ I am ready to face the new day with energy and a good mood.

•••

Put Your Learning to the Test

1. Translate the following sentences using the vocabulary from the story:

a) Je reste dans la salle de bain pendant quelques minutes.

____

b) Je prends un petit-déjeuner rapide.

____

c) Je choisis un t-shirt pour la journée.

____

d) Je bois un grand verre de lait.

____

e) Je prends une douche chaude.

____

2. Rearrange the order of the following words to form a correct sentence:

a) brosse Je dents les me

____

b) salle la Je vais bain de dans

____

c) petit-déjeuner prends Je un rapide

____

3. Translate the following words from the story:

a) travail ________ d) porte-monnaie ________

b) matin ________ e) fenêtre ________

c) clés ________ f) chat ________

4. Determine if the following statements are true or false:

a) _______ Julie gets up immediately after her alarm rings.

b) _______ Julie eats cereal with fresh fruit for breakfast.

c) _______ Julie leaves her apartment at seven o'clock.

d) _______ Julie's cat is named Mina.

Review your answers on the next page.

Answer Key

1. a) I stay in the bathroom for a few minutes.

   b) I have a quick breakfast.

   c) I choose a t-shirt for the day.

   d) I drink a large glass of milk.

   e) I take a hot shower.

2. a) Je me brosse les dents.

   b) Je vais dans la salle de bain.

   c) Je prends un petit-déjeuner rapide.

3. a) work b) morning c) keys

   d) wallet e) window f) cat

4. a) False b) True c) False d) True

Main verb tense:
Present simple
(Présent de l'indicatif)

Main persons:
1st and 2nd person singular
(1ère et 2e personne du singulier)

Text type:
Dialogue
(Dialogue)

Vocabulary theme:
School
(L'école)

Listening to the story is key to mastering pronunciation and an essential step in your learning journey.

- Start with **slow audio** if you need extra clarity.
- Listen at **normal speed** to get used to natural French.
- Challenge yourself with **fast audio** when you're ready.
- **Practice pronunciation:** Pause after each sentence and repeat it out loud!

Find the audio download on page 12.

Conversation à la cafétéria

C'est la pause déjeuner à l'école. Marie et Stéphanie, deux élèves de classes différentes qui viennent de se rencontrer à la cafétéria, discutent de leur journée.

Marie : Salut Stéphanie ! Comment se passe ta journée à l'école aujourd'hui ?

Stéphanie : Bonjour Marie ! Ma journée se passe bien, merci. Et toi, que penses-tu des cours d'aujourd'hui ?

Marie : J'ai beaucoup aimé le cours de français ce matin. Je lis une histoire intéressante. Tu aimes lire en classe ?

Stéphanie : Oui, j'adore lire ! Quel genre d'histoire lis-tu ?

Marie : C'est une histoire d'aventure. Le professeur me pose des questions sur le texte. Je trouve ça amusant. Tu as aussi cours de français aujourd'hui ?

Stéphanie : Non, je n'ai pas français aujourd'hui. J'ai eu mathématiques ce matin. J'apprends les fractions. Tu aimes les maths ?

Marie : Les maths sont un peu difficiles pour moi. Je préfère les langues. Tu peux m'aider avec les fractions ?

Stéphanie : Bien sûr ! Je peux t'expliquer après l'école si tu veux. Que fais-tu après les cours ?

Marie : Merci, c'est gentil ! Après l'école, j'ai une activité de sport. Je joue au volleyball. Et toi, tu as des activités après l'école ?

Stéphanie : Oui, je vais au club de sciences. Je fais des expériences intéressantes. Aujourd'hui, j'étudie les plantes.

Marie : Ça a l'air passionnant ! J'aimerais voir ça. Tu peux me raconter demain ?

Stéphanie : Bien sûr ! Je te raconterai tout. Oh, tu as quel cours cet après-midi ?

Marie : J'ai histoire et puis anglais. Tu aimes l'histoire ?

Stéphanie : Oui, j'adore l'histoire ! J'étudie les Romains en ce moment. C'est fascinant ! Et toi, tu aimes l'anglais ?

Marie : C'est un peu difficile, mais j'essaie de m'améliorer. Tu parles bien anglais ?

Stéphanie : Je me débrouille. Si tu veux, on peut pratiquer ensemble parfois.

Marie : C'est une bonne idée ! Merci Stéphanie. Oh, la cloche sonne. Je dois retourner en classe.

Stéphanie : Tu as raison. Bon courage pour tes cours de l'après-midi, Marie !

Marie : Merci, toi aussi ! À plus tard !

Stéphanie : À plus tard ! Bonne journée !

Explore the Translation

FS ▶ Conversation à la cafétéria
LT/NT ▶ Conversation at the cafeteria

FS ▶ C'est la pause déjeuner à l'école.
LT ▶ It is the break lunch at the school.
▼
NT ▶ It's lunchtime at school.

•••

FS ▶ Marie et Stéphanie, deux élèves de classes différentes qui viennent de se rencontrer à la cafétéria, discutent de leur journée.
LT ▶ Marie and Stéphanie, two students of classes different who come from themselves to meet at the cafeteria, discuss of their day.
▼
NT ▶ Marie and Stéphanie, two students from different classes who

just met in the cafeteria, are talking about their day.

•••

FS ▶ Marie : Salut Stéphanie ! Comment se passe ta journée à l'école aujourd'hui ?

LT ▶ Hi Stéphanie! How itself goes your day at the school today?

NT ▶ Hi Stéphanie! How's your day at school going today?

•••

FS ▶ Stéphanie : Bonjour Marie ! Ma journée se passe bien, merci. Et toi, que penses-tu des cours d'aujourd'hui ?

LT ▶ Hello Marie! My day itself goes well, thanks. And you, what think you of the classes of today?

NT ▶ Hi Marie! My day's going well, thank you. And you, what do you think about today's classes?

•••

FS ▶ Marie : J'ai beaucoup aimé le cours de français ce matin. Je lis une histoire intéressante. Tu aimes lire en classe ?

LT ▶ I have much liked the class of French this morning. I read a story interesting. You like to read in class?

NT ▶ I really liked the French class this morning. I'm reading an interesting story. Do you like reading in class?

•••

FS ▶ Stéphanie : Oui, j'adore lire ! Quel genre d'histoire lis-tu ?

LT ▶ Yes, I love to read! What kind of story read you?

NT ▶ Yes, I love reading! What kind of story are you reading?

•••

FS ▶ Marie : C'est une histoire d'aventure. Le professeur me pose des questions sur le texte. Je trouve ça amusant. Tu as aussi cours de français aujourd'hui ?

LT ▶ It is a story of adventure. The teacher to me asks some questions on the text. I find that fun. You have also class of French today?

▼

NT ▶ It's an adventure story. The teacher asks me questions about the text. I think it's fun. Do you also have French class today?

•••

FS ▶ Stéphanie : Non, je n'ai pas français aujourd'hui. J'ai eu mathématiques ce matin. J'apprends les fractions. Tu aimes les maths ?

LT ▶ No, I have not French today. I had mathematics this morning. I learn the fractions. You like the maths?

▼

NT ▶ No, I don't have French today. I had math this morning. I'm learning fractions. Do you like math?

•••

FS ▶ Marie : Les maths sont un peu difficiles pour moi. Je préfère les langues. Tu peux m'aider avec les fractions ?

LT ▶ The maths are a little difficult for me. I prefer the languages. You can me help with the fractions?

▼

NT ▶ Math is a bit difficult for me. I prefer languages. Can you help me with fractions?

•••

FS ▶ Stéphanie : Bien sûr ! Je peux t'expliquer après l'école si tu veux. Que fais-tu après les cours ?

LT ▶ Well sure! I can to you explain after the school if you want. What do-you after the classes?

▼

NT ▶ Of course! I can explain it to you after school if you want. What

do you do after classes?

•••

FS ▶ Marie : Merci, c'est gentil ! Après l'école, j'ai une activité de sport. Je joue au volleyball. Et toi, tu as des activités après l'école ?

LT ▶ Thank you, it is kind! After the school, I have an activity of sport. I play at volleyball. And you, you have some activities after the school?

▼

NT ▶ Thank you, that's kind of you! After school, I have a sports activity. I play volleyball. And you, do you have activities after school?

•••

FS ▶ Stéphanie : Oui, je vais au club de sciences. Je fais des expériences intéressantes. Aujourd'hui, j'étudie les plantes.

LT ▶ Yes, I go to the club of sciences. I do some experiments interesting. Today, I study the plants.

NT ▶ Yes, I go to the science club. I do interesting experiments. Today, I'm studying plants.

•••

FS▶ Marie : Ça a l'air passionnant ! J'aimerais voir ça. Tu peux me raconter demain ?

LT ▶ That has the air exciting! I would like to see that. You can to me tell tomorrow?

NT ▶ That sounds exciting! I'd love to see that. Can you tell me about it tomorrow?

•••

FS ▶ Stéphanie : Bien sûr ! Je te raconterai tout. Oh, tu as quel cours cet après-midi ?

LT ▶ Well sure! I to you will tell all. Oh, you have which class this afternoon?

NT ▶ Of course! I'll tell you everything. Oh, what class do you have this afternoon?

•••

FS ▶ Marie : J'ai histoire et puis anglais. Tu aimes l'histoire ?

LT ▶ I have history and then English. You like the history?

NT ▶ I have history and then English. Do you like history?

•••

FS ▶ Stéphanie : Oui, j'adore l'histoire ! J'étudie les Romains en ce moment. C'est fascinant ! Et toi, tu aimes l'anglais ?

LT ▶ Yes, I love the history! I study the Romans at this moment. It is fascinating! And you, you like the English?

NT ▶ Yes, I love history! I'm studying the Romans right now. It's fascinating! And you, do you like English?

•••

FS ▶ Marie : C'est un peu difficile, mais j'essaie de m'améliorer. Tu parles bien anglais ?

LT ▶ It is a bit difficult, but I try of myself improve. You speak well English?

NT ▶ It's a bit difficult, but I try to improve myself. Do you speak English well?

•••

FS ▶ Stéphanie : Je me débrouille. Si tu veux, on peut pratiquer ensemble parfois.

LT ▶ I myself manage. If you want, we can practice together sometimes.

NT ▶ I manage. If you want, we can practice together sometimes.

•••

FS ▶ Marie : C'est une bonne idée ! Merci Stéphanie. Oh, la cloche sonne. Je dois retourner en classe.

LT ▶ It is a good idea! Thank you Stéphanie. Oh, the bell rings. I must return in class.

NT ▶ That's a good idea! Thanks, Stéphanie. Oh, the bell is ringing. I have to go back to class.

•••

FS ▶ Stéphanie : Tu as raison. Bon courage pour tes cours de l'après-midi, Marie !

LT ▶ You have reason. Good courage for your classes of the afternoon, Marie!

▼

NT ▶ You're right. Good luck with your afternoon classes, Marie!

•••

FS ▶ Marie : Merci, toi aussi ! À plus tard !

LT ▶ Thank you, you also! See you later!

NT ▶ Thanks, you too! See you later!

•••

FS ▶ Stéphanie : À plus tard ! Bonne journée !

LT ▶ See you later! Good day!

NT ▶ See you later! Have a good day!

•••

Put Your Learning to the Test

1. Translate the following sentences using the vocabulary from the story:

a) Marie adore les cours de langues.

____

b) Stéphanie préfère les sciences aux mathématiques.

____

c) Aujourd'hui, les élèves mangent à la cafétéria.

____

d) Le professeur pose des questions sur l'histoire.

____

2. Rearrange the order of the following words to form a correct sentence:

a) français le classe étudie en J'

____

b) tu après Que fais- école l' ?

____

c) maths trouve difficiles les Marie

____

d) des expériences fait club sciences de au Stéphanie

____

3. Translate the following words from English to French:

a) adventure ___________ d) experiment ___________

b) teacher ___________ e) afternoon ___________

c) story ___________ f) lunch ___________

4. Circle the odd one out:

a) mathématiques - sandwich - sciences - histoire

b) lire - professeur - parler - manger

c) intéressant - élève - professeur - école

d) français - grand - petit - difficile

5. Determine if the following statements are true or false:

a) _______ Marie and Stéphanie have known each other for a long time.

b) _______ Stéphanie finds math easy.

c) _______ Marie prefers languages over math.

d) _______ Stéphanie and Marie eat together every day.

Review your answers on the next page.

Answer Key

1. a) Marie loves language classes.

   b) Stéphanie prefers science over math.

   c) Today, the students eat in the cafeteria.

   d) The teacher asks questions about the story.

2. a) J'étudie le français en classe.

   b) Que fais-tu après l'école ?

   c) Marie trouve les maths difficiles.

   d) Stéphanie fait des expériences au club de sciences.

3. a) aventure b) professeur c) histoire

   d) expérience e) après-midi f) déjeuner

4. a) sandwich
   The other words are school subjects, but a sandwich is food.

   b) professeur
   The other words are actions, but a professor is a person.

   c) intéressant
   The other words are related to school, but "intéressant" is an adjective.

   d) français
   The other words are adjectives, but "français" is a language.

5. a) False b) True c) True d) False

Main verb tense:
Present simple
(Présent de l'indicatif)

Main person:
1st person plural
(1ère personne du pluriel)

Text type:
First-person narrative
(Récit à la première personne)

Vocabulary theme:
Vacation
(Les vacances)

Listening to the story is key to mastering pronunciation and an essential step in your learning journey.

- Start with **slow audio** if you need extra clarity.
- Listen at **normal speed** to get used to natural French.
- Challenge yourself with **fast audio** when you're ready.
- **Practice pronunciation:** Pause after each sentence and repeat it out loud!

Find the audio download on page 12.

Nos vacances d'été

Nous sommes en été et c'est le moment de partir en vacances. Nous sommes une famille de quatre : mes parents, ma petite sœur et moi. Nous aimons beaucoup voyager ensemble.

Cette année, nous décidons de passer deux semaines à la mer. Nous habitons loin de la côte, alors nous prenons la voiture pour y aller. Nous partons tôt le matin, quand il fait encore frais.

Pendant le voyage, nous chantons et nous jouons à des jeux. Nous nous arrêtons parfois pour manger un sandwich et nous reposer un peu. Après plusieurs heures de route, nous arrivons enfin à destination.

Nous louons un petit appartement près de la plage. De nos fenêtres, nous voyons la mer bleue et nous entendons le bruit des vagues. C'est magnifique !

Chaque matin, nous allons à la plage. Nous installons nos serviettes sur le sable chaud et nous mettons de la crème solaire. Ma sœur et moi, nous aimons nager dans la mer. L'eau est fraîche et agréable.

Parfois, nous faisons des châteaux de sable ensemble. Nous ramassons aussi des coquillages pour notre collection. À midi, nous pique-niquons souvent sur la plage. Nous mangeons des sandwichs et des fruits frais.

L'après-midi, nous faisons différentes activités. Un jour, nous faisons une promenade en bateau. Nous voyons des dauphins au loin, c'est très excitant ! Un autre jour, nous visitons un petit village de pêcheurs. Nous goûtons du poisson frais au restaurant, c'est délicieux !

Le soir, nous nous promenons sur la promenade au bord de la mer. Nous mangeons des glaces et nous regardons le coucher de soleil. C'est un moment magique que nous adorons partager en famille.

Pendant notre séjour, nous rencontrons d'autres familles. Nous jouons au ballon sur la plage avec nos nouveaux amis. Nous rions beaucoup et nous nous amusons bien.

Le week-end, nous visitons un parc aquatique. Nous glissons sur les toboggans et nous nageons dans les grandes piscines. C'est une journée pleine d'aventures et de rires.

Malheureusement, les vacances passent trop vite. Bientôt, c'est déjà le moment de rentrer à la maison. Nous faisons nos valises et nous disons au revoir à la mer.

Sur le chemin du retour, nous parlons de tous nos bons souvenirs. Nous sommes un peu tristes de partir, mais nous sommes heureux d'avoir passé ces belles vacances ensemble.

À la maison, nous regardons nos photos et nous montrons nos coquillages à nos amis. Nous avons hâte de revenir l'année prochaine pour de nouvelles aventures au bord de la mer !

Explore the Translation

FS ▶ Nos vacances d'été

LT ▶ Our vacations of summer

NT ▶ Our summer vacation

•••

FS ▶ Nous sommes en été et c'est le moment de partir en vacances.

LT ▶ We are in summer and it is the moment of to leave on vacation.

NT ▶ It's summer, and it's time to go on vacation.

•••

FS ▶ Nous sommes une famille de quatre : mes parents, ma petite sœur et moi.

LT/NT ▶ We are a family of four: my parents, my little sister, and me.

•••

FS ▶ Nous aimons beaucoup voyager ensemble.

LT ▶ We like very much to travel together.

NT ▶ We love traveling together.

•••

FS ▶ Cette année, nous décidons de passer deux semaines à la mer.

LT ▶ This year, we decide to spend two weeks at the sea.

NT ▶ This year, we decided to spend two weeks by the sea.

•••

FS ▶ Nous habitons loin de la côte, alors nous prenons la voiture pour y aller.

LT ▶ We live far from the coast, so we take the car for there to go.

NT ▶ We live far from the coast, so we drive there.

•••

FS ▶ Nous partons tôt le matin, quand il fait encore frais.

LT ▶ We leave early the morning, when it makes still fresh.

NT ▶ We leave early in the morning, while it's still cool.

•••

FS ▶ Pendant le voyage, nous chantons et nous jouons à des jeux.

LT ▶ During the trip, we sing and we play at some games.

▼

NT ▶ During the trip, we sing and play games.

•••

FS ▶ Nous nous arrêtons parfois pour manger un sandwich et nous reposer un peu.

LT ▶ We ourselves stop sometimes for to eat a sandwich and ourselves to rest a bit.

NT ▶ We stop sometimes to eat a sandwich and rest a little.

•••

FS ▶ Après plusieurs heures de route, nous arrivons enfin à destination.

LT ▶ After several hours of road, we arrive finally at destination.

NT ▶ After several hours on the road, we finally arrive at our destination.

•••

FS ▶ Nous louons un petit appartement près de la plage.

LT ▶ We rent a small apartment near of the beach.

NT ▶ We rent a small apartment near the beach.

•••

FS ▶ De nos fenêtres, nous voyons la mer bleue et nous entendons le bruit des vagues. C'est magnifique !

LT ▶ From our windows, we see the sea blue and we hear the sound of the waves. It is magnificent!

NT ▶ From our windows, we see the blue sea and hear the sound of the waves. It's beautiful!

•••

FS ▶ Chaque matin, nous allons à la plage.

LT ▶ Each morning, we go to the beach.

NT ▶ Every morning, we go to the beach.

•••

FS ▶ Nous installons nos serviettes sur le sable chaud et nous mettons de la crème solaire.

LT ▶ We lay our towels on the sand hot and we put on some sunscreen.

NT ▶ We lay our towels on the warm sand and put on sunscreen.

FS ▶ Ma sœur et moi, nous aimons nager dans la mer.L'eau est fraîche et agréable.

LT ▶ My sister and I, we like to swim in the sea. The water is fresh and pleasant.

NT ▶ My sister and I love swimming in the sea. The water is cool and pleasant.

FS ▶ Parfois, nous faisons des châteaux de sable ensemble.

LT ▶ Sometimes, we make some castles of sand together.

NT ▶ Sometimes, we build sandcastles together.

FS ▶ Nous ramassons aussi des coquillages pour notre collection.

LT ▶ We collect also some shells for our collection.

NT ▶ We also collect shells for our collection.

FS ▶ À midi, nous pique-niquons souvent sur la plage.

LT ▶ At noon, we picnic often on the beach.

NT ▶ At noon, we often have picnics on the beach.

FS ▶ Nous mangeons des sandwichs et des fruits frais.

LT ▶ We eat some sandwiches and some fruits fresh.

NT ▶ We eat sandwiches and fresh fruit.

•••

FS ▶ L'après-midi, nous faisons différentes activités. Un jour, nous faisons une promenade en bateau.

LT ▶ The afternoon, we do different activities. One day, we make an outing in boat.

▼

NT ▶ In the afternoon, we do various activities. One day, we take a boat ride.

•••

FS ▶ Nous voyons des dauphins au loin, c'est très excitant !

LT ▶ We see some dolphins in the distance, it is very exciting!

▼

NT ▶ We see dolphins in the distance. It's very exciting!

•••

FS ▶ Un autre jour, nous visitons un petit village de pêcheurs.

LT ▶ Another day, we visit a small village of fishermen.

▼

NT ▶ Another day, we visit a small fishing village.

•••

FS ▶ Nous goûtons du poisson frais au restaurant, c'est délicieux !

LT ▶ We taste some fish fresh at the restaurant, it is delicious!

▼

NT ▶ We taste fresh fish at the restaurant. It's delicious!

•••

FS ▶ Le soir, nous nous promenons sur la promenade au bord de la mer.

LT ▶ The evening, we ourselves walk on the boardwalk at the edge of the sea.

▼

NT ▶ In the evening, we walk along the seaside boardwalk.

•••

FS ▶ Nous mangeons des glaces et nous regardons le coucher de soleil.

LT ▶ We eat some ice creams and we watch the setting of sun.

NT ▶ We eat ice cream and watch the sunset.

•••

FS ▶ C'est un moment magique que nous adorons partager en famille.

LT ▶ It is a moment magical that we love to share as a family.

NT ▶ It's a magical moment we love to share as a family.

•••

FS ▶ Pendant notre séjour, nous rencontrons d'autres familles.

LT/NT ▶ During our stay, we meet other families.

•••

FS ▶ Nous jouons au ballon sur la plage avec nos nouveaux amis.

LT ▶ We play at the ball on the beach with our new friends.

NT ▶ We play ball on the beach with our new friends.

•••

FS ▶ Nous rions beaucoup et nous nous amusons bien.

LT ▶ We laugh a lot and we ourselves have fun well.

▼

NT ▶ We laugh a lot and have a great time.

•••

FS ▶ Le week-end, nous visitons un parc aquatique.

LT ▶ The weekend, we visit a park aquatic.

▼

NT ▶ On the weekend, we visit a water park.

•••

FS ▶ Nous glissons sur les toboggans et nous nageons dans les grandes piscines.

LT ▶ We slide on the slides and we swim in the big pools.

NT ▶ We slide down the water slides and swim in the large pools.

•••

FS ▶ C'est une journée pleine d'aventures et de rires.

LT ▶ It is a day full of adventures and of laughter.

NT ▶ It's a day full of adventures and laughter.

•••

FS ▶ Malheureusement, les vacances passent trop vite.

LT ▶ Unfortunately, the vacations pass too fast.

NT ▶ Unfortunately, vacations go by too quickly.

•••

FS ▶ Bientôt, c'est déjà le moment de rentrer à la maison.

LT ▶ Soon, it is already the moment to return to the house.

NT ▶ Soon, it's already time to go home.

•••

FS ▶ Nous faisons nos valises et nous disons au revoir à la mer.

LT ▶ We make our suitcases and we say goodbye to the sea.

NT ▶ We pack our bags and say goodbye to the sea.

•••

FS ▶ Sur le chemin du retour, nous parlons de tous nos bons souvenirs.

LT ▶ On the way of return, we talk about all our good memories.

NT ▶ On the way back, we talk about all our good memories.

•••

FS ▶ Nous sommes un peu tristes de partir, mais nous sommes heureux d'avoir passé ces belles vacances ensemble.

LT ▶ We are a little sad to leave, but we are happy to have spent these beautiful vacations together.

NT ▶ We're a little sad to leave, but we're happy to have spent this wonderful vacation together.

•••

FS ▶ À la maison, nous regardons nos photos et nous montrons nos coquillages à nos amis.

LT ▶ At the house, we look at our photos and we show our shells to our friends.

NT ▶ At home, we look at our photos and show our seashells to our friends.

•••

FS ▶ Nous avons hâte de revenir l'année prochaine pour de nouvelles aventures au bord de la mer !

LT ▶ We have haste to return the year next for some new adventures at the edge of the sea!

NT ▶ We can't wait to come back next year for new seaside adventures!

•••

Put Your Learning to the Test

1. Translate the following sentences using the vocabulary from the story:

    a) Nous nous réveillons tôt pour partir quand il fait encore frais.

    ____

    b) Les enfants construisent des châteaux de sable sur la plage.

    ____

    c) Nous faisons une promenade en bateau et nous voyons des dauphins.

    ____

    d) Chaque soir, nous nous promenons sur la promenade au bord de la mer.

    ____

2. Rearrange the order of the following words to form a correct sentence:

    a) la plage allons Nous à matin chaque

    ____

    b) de louons Nous près un la appartement mer

    ____

    c) faisons promenade une bateau en Nous

    ____

    d) toujours vacances Les passent vite

    ____

3. Why does the family wake up early on the day of departure?

   a) Because they have a long drive ahead.

   b) Because they want to see the sunrise at the beach.

   c) Because they have to catch a plane.

   d) Because they like to eat breakfast very early.

4. Complete the sentences with the correct word from the list:

Words: coucher de soleil, dauphins, sable, pique-nique

Use each word only once

   a) L'après-midi, nous préparons un ____________ avec des sandwichs et des fruits.

   b) Les enfants jouent avec le ____________ en construisant des châteaux sur la plage.

   c) Pendant notre promenade en bateau, nous avons eu la chance de voir des ____________ au loin

   d) Le soir, nous aimons regarder le magnifique ____________ au bord de l'océan.

5. Determine if the following statements are true or false:

   a) ______ The family goes to the sea every summer.

   b) ______ They travel by train to their destination.

   c) ______ The children collect seashells on the beach.

   d) ______ They visit a fishing village and eat fresh seafood.

Review your answers on the next page.

Answer Key

1. a) We wake up early to leave when it is still cool.
   b) The children build sandcastles on the beach.
   c) We take a boat trip and see dolphins.
   d) Every evening, we walk along the seaside promenade.

2. a) Nous allons à la plage chaque matin.
   b) Nous louons un appartement près de la mer.
   c) Nous faisons une promenade en bateau.
   d) Les vacances passent toujours vite.

3. a) Because they have a long drive ahead.

4. a) pique-nique b) sable
   c) dauphins d) coucher de soleil

5. a) False b) False c) True d) True

Main verb tense:
Present simple
(Présent de l'indicatif)

Main persons:
1st person singular, 3rd person singular and plural
(1ère personne du singulier, 3ème personne du singulier et du pluriel)

Text type:
Descriptive narrative
(Récit descriptif)

Vocabulary theme:
Family members
(Membres de la famille)

Listening to the story is key to mastering pronunciation and an essential step in your learning journey.

- Start with **slow audio** if you need extra clarity.
- Listen at **normal speed** to get used to natural French.
- Challenge yourself with **fast audio** when you're ready.
- **Practice pronunciation:** Pause after each sentence and repeat it out loud!

Find the audio download on page 12.

Présentation de ma famille

Bonjour ! Je m'appelle Marc et j'ai 30 ans. Aujourd'hui, je veux te parler de ma famille. Elle est très unie et je l'aime beaucoup.

Commençons par mes parents. Mon père s'appelle François. Il a 60 ans et il est boulanger. Il se lève très tôt chaque matin pour faire le meilleur pain de la ville. Ma mère s'appelle Marie. Elle a 58 ans et elle est institutrice dans une école primaire. Elle adore les enfants et s'inquiète toujours pour tout le monde.

J'ai un grand frère, Thomas. Il a 35 ans, il est marié et a deux enfants. Il travaille comme ingénieur. Thomas est très intelligent et m'aide souvent quand j'ai un problème. Ma petite sœur Sophie a 25 ans. Elle étudie la médecine et veut devenir docteur comme notre grand-père.

Parlons de mes grands-parents. Mon grand-père paternel, Pierre, a 85 ans. Il était médecin mais est maintenant à la retraite. Il aime raconter des histoires sur son ancien métier. Ma grand-mère Jeanne a 82 ans et fait les meilleures tartes aux pommes du monde ! Mes grands-parents maternels, Paul et Claire, ne sont plus là, mais nous pensons souvent à eux. Ils me manquent beaucoup.

J'ai aussi un oncle et une tante du côté de ma mère. Mon oncle Luc est le frère de ma mère. Il est très drôle et fait toujours des blagues. Ma tante Anne est artiste et peint de beaux tableaux.

J'ai plusieurs cousins et cousines. Léa a 28 ans et est journaliste. Elle voyage beaucoup. Émile a 26 ans et est pompier. Il est très courageux. Ma petite cousine Julie a 18 ans et vient de commencer ses études à l'université.

Les enfants de mon frère Thomas sont Lucas, 5 ans, et Emma, 3 ans. Ils sont adorables et pleins d'énergie. J'adore jouer avec eux quand je leur rends visite. La dernière arrivée dans notre famille est ma nièce Chloé, le bébé de ma sœur Sophie. Elle a seulement 6 mois et sourit tout le temps. Toute la famille est folle d'elle !

Notre famille est grande et importante pour nous. Nous nous réunissons souvent pour des repas de famille. C'est toujours un moment joyeux avec beaucoup de rires et de bons souvenirs. Les enfants jouent ensemble, les adultes discutent, et tout le monde profite de la délicieuse cuisine de ma grand-mère.

Ces moments en famille sont précieux. Ils nous rappellent l'importance des liens familiaux et renforcent notre amour les uns pour les autres. Malgré nos différences d'âge et nos vies bien remplies, nous trouvons toujours du temps pour être ensemble et partager notre bonheur.

Explore the Translation

FS ▶ Présenation de ma famille

LT ▶ Presentation of my family

▼

NT ▶ Introducing my family

FS ▶ Bonjour ! Je m'appelle Marc et j'ai 30 ans.

LT ▶ Hello! I myself call Marc and I have 30 years.

▼

NT ▶ Hello! My name is Marc, and I'm 30 years old.

FS ▶ Aujourd'hui, je veux te parler de ma famille.

LT ▶ Today, I want to you talk about my family.

▼

NT ▶ Today, I want to tell you about my family.

FS ▶ Elle est très unie et je l'aime beaucoup.

LT ▶ She is very united, and I it love a lot.

▼

NT ▶ It's very close-knit, and I love it a lot.

FS ▶ Commençons par mes parents.

LT ▶ Let's begin by my parents.
▼
NT ▶ Let's start with my parents.

•••

FS ▶ Mon père s'appelle François.
LT ▶ My father himself calls François.
▼
NT ▶ My father's name is François.

•••

FS ▶ Il a 60 ans et il est boulanger.
LT ▶ He has 60 years and he is baker.
▼
NT ▶ He's 60 years old, and he's a baker.

•••

FS ▶ Il se lève très tôt chaque matin pour faire le meilleur pain de la ville.
LT ▶ He himself gets up very early each morning to make the best bread of the city.
▼
NT ▶ He gets up very early every morning to make the best bread in town.

•••

FS ▶ Ma mère s'appelle Marie.
LT ▶ My mother herself calls Marie.
▼
NT ▶ My mother's name is Marie.

•••

FS ▶ Elle a 58 ans et elle est institutrice dans une école primaire.
LT ▶ She has 58 years, and she is teacher in a school primary.

▼

NT ▶ She's 58 years old, and she's a teacher at a primary school.

•••

FS ▶ Elle adore les enfants et s'inquiète toujours pour tout le monde.

LT ▶ She loves the children and herself worries always for all the world.

NT ▶ She loves children and always worries about everyone.

•••

FS ▶ J'ai un grand frère, Thomas.

LT ▶ I have a big brother, Thomas.

NT ▶ I have an older brother, Thomas.

•••

FS ▶ Il a 35 ans, il est marié et a deux enfants.

LT ▶ He has 35 years, he is married and has two children.

NT ▶ He's 35 years old, married, and has two children.

•••

FS ▶ Il travaille comme ingénieur.

LT ▶ He works as engineer.

NT ▶ He works as an engineer.

•••

FS ▶ Thomas est très intelligent et m'aide souvent quand j'ai un problème.

LT ▶ Thomas is very intelligent and me helps often when I have a problem.

▼

NT ▶ Thomas is very smart and often helps me when I have a problem.

•••

FS ▶ Ma petite sœur Sophie a 25 ans.

LT ▶ My little sister Sophie has 25 years.

▼

NT ▶ My little sister Sophie is 25 years old.

•••

FS ▶ Elle étudie la médecine et veut devenir docteur comme notre grand-père.

LT ▶ She studies the medicine and wants to become doctor like our grandfather.

NT ▶ She studies medicine and wants to become a doctor like our grandfather.

•••

FS ▶ Parlons de mes grands-parents.

LT/NT ▶ Let's talk about my grandparents.

•••

FS ▶ Mon grand-père paternel, Pierre, a 85 ans.

LT ▶ My grandfather paternal, Pierre, has 85 years.

NT ▶ My paternal grandfather, Pierre, is 85 years old.

•••

FS ▶ Il était médecin mais est maintenant à la retraite.

LT ▶ He was doctor but is now at the retirement.

NT ▶ He was a doctor but is now retired.

•••

FS ▶ Il aime raconter des histoires sur son ancien métier.

LT ▶ He likes to tell some stories on his former profession.

▼

NT ▶ He likes telling stories about his former profession.

•••

FS ▶ Ma grand-mère Jeanne a 82 ans et fait les meilleures tartes aux pommes du monde !

LT ▶ My grandmother Jeanne has 82 years and makes the best pies of apples of the world!

NT ▶ My grandmother Jeanne is 82 years old and makes the best apple pies in the world!

•••

FS ▶ Mes grands-parents maternels, Paul et Claire, ne sont plus là, mais nous pensons souvent à eux.

LT ▶ My grandparents maternal, Paul and Claire, are no longer there, but we think often of them.

NT ▶ My maternal grandparents, Paul and Claire, are no longer with us, but we often think of them.

•••

FS ▶ Ils me manquent beaucoup.

LT ▶ They me are missing a lot.

NT ▶ I miss them a lot.

•••

FS ▶ J'ai aussi un oncle et une tante du côté de ma mère.

LT ▶ I have also an uncle and an aunt on the side of my mother.

▼

NT ▶ I also have an uncle and an aunt on my mother's side.

•••

FS ▶ Mon oncle Luc est le frère de ma mère.
LT ▶ My uncle Luc is the brother of my mother.
▼
NT ▶ My uncle Luc is my mother's brother.

•••

FS ▶ Il est très drôle et fait toujours des blagues.
LT ▶ He is very funny and makes always some jokes.

NT ▶ He's very funny and always makes jokes.

•••

FS ▶ Ma tante Anne est artiste et peint de beaux tableaux.
LT ▶ My aunt Anne is artist and paints some beautiful paintings.

NT ▶ My aunt Anne is an artist and paints beautiful paintings.

•••

FS ▶ J'ai plusieurs cousins et cousines.
LT/NT ▶ I have several cousins.

•••

FS ▶ Léa a 28 ans et est journaliste.
LT ▶ Léa has 28 years and is journalist.

NT ▶ Léa is 28 years old and is a journalist.

•••

FS ▶ Elle voyage beaucoup.
LT/NT ▶ She travels a lot.

•••

FS ▶ Émile a 26 ans et est pompier.

LT ▶ Émile has 26 years and is firefighter.

▼

NT ▶ Émile is 26 years old and is a firefighter.

•••

FS ▶ Il est très courageux.

LT ▶ He is very courageous.

▼

NT ▶ He is very brave.

•••

FS ▶ Ma petite cousine Julie a 18 ans et vient de commencer ses études à l'université.

LT ▶ My little cousin Julie has 18 years and comes of start her studies at the university.

NT ▶ My younger cousin Julie is 18 years old and has just started her university studies.

•••

FS ▶ Les enfants de mon frère Thomas sont Lucas, 5 ans, et Emma, 3 ans.

LT ▶ The children of my brother Thomas are Lucas, 5 years, and Emma, 3 years.

NT ▶ My brother Thomas's children are Lucas, 5 years old, and Emma, 3 years old.

•••

FS ▶ Ils sont adorables et pleins d'énergie.

LT/NT ▶ They are adorable and full of energy.

•••

FS ▶ J'adore jouer avec eux quand je leur rends visite.

LT ▶ I love to play with them when I to them make visit.

▼

NT ▶ I love playing with them when I visit them.

•••

FS ▶ La dernière arrivée dans notre famille est ma nièce Chloé, le bébé de ma sœur Sophie.

LT ▶ The last arrival in our family is my niece Chloé, the baby of my sister Sophie.

▼

NT ▶ The newest addition to our family is my niece Chloé, my sister Sophie's baby.

•••

FS ▶ Elle a seulement 6 mois et sourit tout le temps.

LT ▶ She has only 6 months and smiles all the time.

NT ▶ She is only 6 months old and smiles all the time.

•••

FS ▶ Toute la famille est folle d'elle !

LT ▶ All the family is crazy of her!

NT ▶ The whole family adores her!

•••

FS ▶ Notre famille est grande et importante pour nous.

LT ▶ Our family is big and important for us.

NT ▶ Our family is large and important to us.

•••

FS ▶ Nous nous réunissons souvent pour des repas de famille.

LT ▶ We ourselves gather often for some meals of family .

▼

NT ▶ We often get together for family meals.

•••

FS ▶ C'est toujours un moment joyeux avec beaucoup de rires et de bons souvenirs.

LT ▶ It is always a moment joyful with lots of laughter and good memories.

▼

NT ▶ It's always a joyful time filled with laughter and good memories.

•••

FS ▶ Les enfants jouent ensemble, les adultes discutent, et tout le monde profite de la délicieuse cuisine de ma grand-mère.

LT ▶ The children play together, the adults discuss, and all the world enjoys the delicious cooking of my grandmother.

▼

NT ▶ The children play together, the adults talk, and everyone enjoys my grandmother's delicious cooking.

•••

FS ▶ Ces moments en famille sont précieux.

LT ▶ These moments in family are precious.

▼

NT ▶ These family moments are precious.

•••

FS ▶ Ils nous rappellent l'importance des liens familiaux et renforcent notre amour les uns pour les autres.

LT ▶ They to us remind the importance of links family and strengthen our love the ones for the others.

▼

NT ▶ They remind us of the importance of family bonds and strengthen our love for one another.

•••

FS ▶ Malgré nos différences d'âge et nos vies bien remplies, nous trouvons toujours du temps pour être ensemble et partager notre bonheur.

LT ▶ Despite our differences of age and our lives well filled, we find always some time to be together and share our happiness.

▼

NT ▶ Despite our age differences and busy lives, we always find time to be together and share our happiness.

•••

Put Your Learning to the Test

1. Translate the following sentences using the vocabulary from the story:

a) Mon père se lève tôt pour préparer du pain.

____

b) Mon grand-père aime raconter des histoires sur son ancien métier.

____

c) Mon cousin est pompier, c'est un travail difficile et courageux.

____

d) Toute la famille se réunit souvent pour partager de bons repas.

____

2. Rearrange the order of the following words to form a correct sentence:

a) famille Ma très est unie

____

b) m’appelle Je Marc et trente j’ai ans

____

c) frère Mon travaille comme ingénieur

____

d) Nous réunissons repas nous souvent pour des famille de

____

3. Translate the following words from French to English:

a) boulanger ____________ d) école ____________

b) médecin ____________ e) retraite ____________

c) famille ____________ f) souvenirs ____________

4. Complete the sentences with the correct word from the list:

Words: grand-père, boulangerie, enfants, ingénieur

Use each word only once

a) Mon frère est très intelligent et travaille comme ____________.

b) Mon ____________ était médecin avant de prendre sa retraite.

c) La ____________ prépare les meilleures tartes aux pommes.

d) Mon cousin Thomas a deux ____________ adorables.

5. Determine if the following statements are true or false:

a) _______ Marc has a sister who studies medicine.

b) _______ His grandfather Pierre is a baker.

c) _______ Thomas has three children.

d) _______ The whole family loves to gather for meals.

Review your answers on the next page.

Answer Key

1. a) My father wakes up early to prepare bread.

   b) My grandfather loves telling stories about his former job.

   c) My cousin is a firefighter; it's a tough and courageous job.

   d) The whole family often gathers to share good meals.

2. a) Ma famille est très unie.

   b) Je m’appelle Marc et j’ai trente ans.

   c) Mon frère travaille comme ingénieur.

   d) Nous nous réunissons souvent pour des repas de famille.

3. a) baker b) doctor c) family

   d) school e) retirement f) memories

4. a) ingénieur b) grand-père

   c) boulangerie d) enfants

5. a) True b) False c) False d) True

Main verb tense:
Present simple
(Présent de l'indicatif)

Main persons:
1st and 3rd person singular
(1ère et 3e personne du singulier)

Text type:
Descriptive narrative
(Récit descriptif)

Vocabulary theme:
Home
(La maison)

Listening to the story is key to mastering pronunciation and an essential step in your learning journey.

- Start with **slow audio** if you need extra clarity.
- Listen at **normal speed** to get used to natural French.
- Challenge yourself with **fast audio** when you're ready.
- **Practice pronunciation:** Pause after each sentence and repeat it out loud!

Find the audio download on page 12.

Ma maison et mon quartier

J'habite dans une jolie maison qui se trouve dans un quartier calme de la ville. Ma maison n'est pas très grande, mais elle est confortable et accueillante. C'est une maison à deux étages que j'ai achetée il y a cinq ans.

Au rez-de-chaussée, il y a un salon spacieux que j'adore. C'est la pièce où je passe le plus de temps. Dans le salon, j'ai un grand canapé confortable et une table basse en bois. Il y a aussi une télévision que je ne regarde pas souvent. Je préfère lire les livres que j'emprunte à la bibliothèque du quartier.

À côté du salon, il y a une cuisine ouverte. Elle n'est pas très grande, mais elle est bien équipée. J'ai un réfrigérateur, une cuisinière et un lave-vaisselle qui me facilitent la vie. Sur le comptoir, il y a une machine à café que j'utilise tous les matins.

À l'étage, il y a trois chambres. Ma chambre est la plus grande. Elle a un grand lit douillet et une armoire où je range mes vêtements. La deuxième chambre sert de bureau. C'est là que je travaille quand je ne vais pas au bureau. La troisième chambre est une chambre d'amis que j'ai décorée avec soin pour accueillir ma famille et mes amis.

Il y a aussi une salle de bain à l'étage. Elle a une baignoire que j'utilise pour me détendre après une longue journée de travail. Je n'ai pas de douche séparée, mais ça ne me dérange pas.

Dans le jardin derrière la maison, j'ai planté des fleurs et des légumes. C'est un petit coin de nature que j'apprécie beaucoup. J'ai aussi installé une table et des chaises où je prends mes repas quand il fait beau.

Mon quartier est très agréable. Il y a un parc à deux pas de chez moi où je vais souvent me promener. C'est un endroit que j'aime particulièrement. Le quartier a aussi plusieurs petits commerces : une boulangerie qui fait du bon pain, une épicerie où je fais mes achats, et un café où je retrouve parfois mes amis.

Je ne suis pas la seule à aimer ma maison. J'ai deux animaux de compagnie qui l'adorent aussi. Mon lapin, Pompon, qui est très curieux, aime se promener librement dans le salon et grignoter les carottes que je lui donne. Mon chien, Rex, est plus énergique. C'est un labrador qui adore jouer dans le jardin et qui m'accompagne lors de mes promenades dans le parc.

Ma maison n'est peut-être pas parfaite, mais c'est mon chez-moi. Je l'ai aménagée avec des meubles et des objets que j'aime, et elle reflète ma personnalité. Avec mon quartier tranquille et mes animaux de compagnie, j'ai créé un environnement où je me sens bien et en sécurité.

Explore the Translation

FS ▶ Ma maison et mon quartier
LT/NT ▶ My house and my neighborhood

•••

FS ▶ J'habite dans une jolie maison qui se trouve dans un quartier calme de la ville.
LT ▶ I live in a pretty house that itself is found in a neighborhood calm of the city.
▼
NT ▶ I live in a pretty house located in a quiet neighborhood in the city.

•••

FS ▶ Ma maison n'est pas très grande, mais elle est confortable et accueillante.
LT ▶ My house is not very big, but it is comfortable and welcoming.
▼
NT ▶ My house isn't very big, but it's comfortable and welcoming.

•••

FS ▶ C'est une maison à deux étages que j'ai achetée il y a cinq ans.
LT ▶ It is a house with two floors that I have bought there are five years.
▼
NT ▶ It's a two-story house that I bought five years ago.

•••

FS ▶ Au rez-de-chaussée, il y a un salon spacieux que j'adore.
LT ▶ On the ground floor, there is a living room spacious that I love.
▼
NT ▶ On the ground floor, there's a spacious living room that I love.

•••

FS ▶ C'est la pièce où je passe le plus de temps.
LT ▶ It is the room where I spend the most of time.
▼
NT ▶ It's the room where I spend most of my time.

•••

FS ▶ Dans le salon, j'ai un grand canapé confortable et une table basse en bois.
LT ▶ In the living room, I have a big couch comfortable and a table low in wood.
▼
NT ▶ In the living room, I have a big comfortable couch and a wooden coffee table.

•••

FS ▶ Il y a aussi une télévision que je ne regarde pas souvent.
LT ▶ There is also a television that I watch not often.
▼
NT ▶ There's also a TV that I don't watch often.

•••

FS ▶ Je préfère lire les livres que j'emprunte à la bibliothèque du quartier.
LT ▶ I prefer to read the books that I borrow at the library of the neighborhood.
▼
NT ▶ I prefer reading the books I borrow from the neighborhood

library.

•••

FS ▶ À côté du salon, il y a une cuisine ouverte.
LT ▶ Next to the living room, there is a kitchen open.
▼
NT ▶ Next to the living room, there's an open kitchen.

•••

FS ▶ Elle n'est pas très grande, mais elle est bien équipée.
LT ▶ It is not very big, but it is well equipped.
▼
NT ▶ It's not very big, but it's well-equipped.

•••

FS ▶ J'ai un réfrigérateur, une cuisinière et un lave-vaisselle qui me facilitent la vie.
LT ▶ I have a refrigerator, a stove, and a dishwasher that me facilitate the life.
▼
NT ▶ I have a refrigerator, a stove, and a dishwasher that make my life easier.

•••

FS ▶ Sur le comptoir, il y a une machine à café que j'utilise tous les matins.
LT ▶ On the counter, there is a machine of coffee that I use every morning.
▼
NT ▶ On the counter, there's a coffee machine that I use every morning.

•••

FS ▶ À l'étage, il y a trois chambres. Ma chambre est la plus grande.
LT ▶ At the floor, there are three bedrooms. My bedroom is the most big.
▼

NT ▶ Upstairs, there are three bedrooms. My bedroom is the biggest.

•••

FS ▶ Elle a un grand lit douillet et une armoire où je range mes vêtements.

LT ▶ It has a big bed cozy and a wardrobe where I store my clothes.

▼

NT ▶ It has a big cozy bed and a wardrobe where I store my clothes.

•••

FS ▶ La deuxième chambre sert de bureau.

LT ▶ The second bedroom serves as office.

▼

NT ▶ The second bedroom serves as an office.

•••

FS ▶ C'est là que je travaille quand je ne vais pas au bureau.

LT ▶ It is there that I work when I not go to the office.

▼

NT ▶ That's where I work when I don't go to the office.

•••

FS ▶ La troisième chambre est une chambre d'amis que j'ai décorée avec soin pour accueillir ma famille et mes amis.

LT ▶ The third bedroom is a bedroom of friends that I have decorated with care to welcome my family and my friends.

▼

NT ▶ The third bedroom is a guest room that I've carefully decorated to welcome my family and friends.

•••

FS ▶ Il y a aussi une salle de bain à l'étage.

LT ▶ There is also a bathroom at the floor.

NT ▶ There's also a bathroom upstairs.

•••

FS ▶ Elle a une baignoire que j'utilise pour me détendre après une longue journée de travail.

LT ▶ It has a bathtub that I use to myself relax after a long day of work.

▼

NT ▶ It has a bathtub that I use to relax after a long workday.

•••

FS ▶ Je n'ai pas de douche séparée, mais ça ne me dérange pas.

LT ▶ I have not a shower separated, but that me bother not.

NT ▶ I don't have a separate shower, but it doesn't bother me.

•••

FS ▶ Dans le jardin derrière la maison, j'ai planté des fleurs et des légumes.

LT ▶ In the garden behind the house, I have planted some flowers and some vegetables.

NT ▶ In the garden behind the house, I've planted flowers and vegetables.

•••

FS ▶ C'est un petit coin de nature que j'apprécie beaucoup.

LT ▶ It is a small corner of nature that I appreciate a lot.

NT ▶ It's a little patch of nature that I really enjoy.

•••

FS ▶ J'ai aussi installé une table et des chaises où je prends mes repas quand il fait beau.

LT ▶ I have also installed a table and some chairs where I take my meals when it makes nice.

NT ▶ I've also set up a table and chairs where I eat when the weather is nice.

•••

FS ▶ Mon quartier est très agréable.

LT ▶ My neighborhood is very pleasant.

NT ▶ My neighborhood is very nice.

•••

FS ▶ Il y a un parc à deux pas de chez moi où je vais souvent me promener.

LT ▶ There is a park at two steps from my home where I go often myself walk.

NT ▶ There's a park just steps from my house where I often go for a walk.

•••

FS ▶ C'est un endroit que j'aime particulièrement.

LT ▶ It is a place that I love particularly.

NT ▶ It's a place I especially love.

•••

FS ▶ Le quartier a aussi plusieurs petits commerces : une boulangerie qui fait du bon pain, une épicerie où je fais mes achats, et un café où je retrouve parfois mes amis.

LT ▶ The neighborhood has also several small shops: a bakery that makes some good bread, a grocery where I do my shopping, and a café where I meet sometimes my friends.

▼

NT ▶ The neighborhood also has several small shops: a bakery that makes great bread, a grocery store where I do my shopping, and a café where I sometimes meet my friends.

•••

FS ▶ Je ne suis pas la seule à aimer ma maison.

LT ▶ I am not the only one to like my house.

▼

NT ▶ I'm not the only one who loves my house.

•••

FS ▶ J'ai deux animaux de compagnie qui l'adorent aussi.

LT ▶ I have two animals of company that it adore also.

▼

NT ▶ I have two pets who love it too.

•••

FS ▶ Mon lapin, Pompon, qui est très curieux, aime se promener librement dans le salon et grignoter les carottes que je lui donne.

LT ▶ My rabbit, Pompon, who is very curious, likes himself to walk freely in the living room and nibble the carrots that I to him give.

▼

NT ▶ My rabbit, Pompon, who's very curious, likes to roam freely in the living room and nibble on the carrots I give him.

•••

FS ▶ Mon chien, Rex, est plus énergique.

LT/NT ▶ My dog, Rex, is more energetic.

•••

FS ▶ C'est un labrador qui adore jouer dans le jardin et qui m'accompagne lors de mes promenades dans le parc.

LT ▶ It is a labrador that loves to play in the garden and that to me accompanies during my walks in the park.

▼

NT ▶ He's a labrador who loves playing in the garden and accompanies me on my walks in the park.

•••

FS ▶ Ma maison n'est peut-être pas parfaite, mais c'est mon chez-moi.

LT ▶ My house is maybe not perfect, but it is my home.

▼

NT ▶ My house might not be perfect, but it's my home.

•••

FS ▶ Je l'ai aménagée avec des meubles et des objets que j'aime, et elle reflète ma personnalité.

LT ▶ I it have furnished with some furniture and some objects that I love, and it reflects my personality.

▼

NT ▶ I've furnished it with furniture and objects I love, and it reflects my personality.

•••

FS ▶ Avec mon quartier tranquille et mes animaux de compagnie, j'ai créé un environnement où je me sens bien et en sécurité.

LT ▶ With my neighborhood quiet and my animals of company, I have created an environment where I myself feel good and in security.

▼

NT ▶ With my quiet neighborhood and my pets, I've created an environment where I feel good and safe.

•••

Put Your Learning to the Test

1. Translate the following sentences using the vocabulary from the story:

    a) Ma maison est située dans un quartier calme et agréable.

    ____

    b) Dans le salon, j'ai un grand canapé confortable.

    ____

    c) J'adore lire les livres que j'emprunte à la bibliothèque.

    ____

    d) Mon chien aime courir et jouer dans le parc.

    ____

2. Rearrange the order of the following words to form a correct sentence:

    a) quartier un habite dans J' calme

    ____

    b) trois étage chambres y a l' Il à

    ____

    c) réfrigérateur un dans cuisine ma ai J'

    ____

    d) Je souvent promener parc me vais au.

    ____

3. What is the narrator's favorite room in the house?

a) The kitchen

b) The bedroom

c) The living room

d) The office

4. Complete the sentences with the correct word from the list:

Words: réfrigérateur, bureau, baignoire, cuisine

Use each word only once

a) La ____________ est équipée d'un lave-vaisselle moderne.

b) Je travaille dans mon ____________ quand je ne vais pas au bureau.

c) Après une longue journée, je me détends dans la ____________.

d) Dans la cuisine, j'ai un ____________ pour conserver mes aliments frais.

5. Determine if the following statements are true or false:

a) ______ The narrator's house is very large and modern.

b) ______ The living room has a comfortable couch and a wooden coffee table.

c) ______ The narrator has a separate shower in the bathroom.

d) ______ There is a park near the narrator's house.

Review your answers on the next page.

Answer Key

1. a) My house is located in a quiet and pleasant neighborhood.

   b) In the living room, I have a large comfortable couch.

   c) I love reading the books I borrow from the library.

   d) My dog loves running and playing in the park.

2. a) J'habite dans un quartier calme.

   b) Il y a trois chambres à l'étage.

   c) J'ai un réfrigérateur dans ma cuisine.

   d) Je vais souvent me promener au parc.

3. c) The living room.

4. a) cuisine b) bureau

   c) baignoire d) réfrigérateur

5. a) False b) True c) False d) True

Main verb tense:
Present simple
(Présent de l'indicatif)

Main persons:
1st person singular, 3rd person singular and plural
(1ère personne du singulier, 3ème personne du singulier et du pluriel)

Text type:
Sports report
(Reportage sportif)

Vocabulary theme:
Sports
(Le sport)

Listening to the story is key to mastering pronunciation and an essential step in your learning journey.

- Start with **slow audio** if you need extra clarity.
- Listen at **normal speed** to get used to natural French.
- Challenge yourself with **fast audio** when you're ready.
- **Practice pronunciation:** Pause after each sentence and repeat it out loud!

Find the audio download on page 12.

Un match de tennis passionnant

Je suis au bord du terrain principal pour vous faire vivre ce match exceptionnel. L'ambiance est excitante ! Les spectateurs s'installent bruyamment dans les gradins. Vont-ils voir un match important ?

Les deux joueurs entrent sur le terrain. Ils saluent le public qui les applaudit fort. Chacun prend sa raquette et commence à s'échauffer. Ils frappent la balle avec force, se préparant pour le match à venir.

L'arbitre appelle les joueurs. Ils se placent de chaque côté du filet. Le premier service est lancé ! La balle passe au-dessus du filet très vite. Le receveur la renvoie avec difficulté. Les échanges sont rapides et forts. Les joueurs courent, glissent, frappent. Ils ne laissent rien passer.

Le public ne fait pas de bruit. Chaque point est important. Les spectateurs encouragent leurs favoris. "Allez !" crient-ils avec joie. L'ambiance est très bonne.

Un joueur marque un point superbe. La foule crie de joie ! Les applaudissements sont forts dans tout le stade. Le joueur lève le poing pour montrer sa joie. Son adversaire, lui, secoue la tête, triste. Mais le match n'est pas fini.

Les jeux continuent. Les joueurs ne semblent pas fatigués. Ils continuent à jouer avec la même force. Leurs coups sont précis et forts. La balle vole d'un côté à l'autre du terrain très vite.

Soudain, un coup droit excellent ! La balle frôle la ligne. Est-elle dedans ou dehors ? L'arbitre annonce : "Dedans !". Le point est bon. Quelle tension !

Le match est serré. Aucun des joueurs ne veut perdre. Ils se battent pour chaque point. Le public regarde sans bouger. Personne ne veut partir. Qui va gagner ?

Les échanges deviennent de plus en plus longs. Les joueurs frappent la balle encore et encore. Ils glissent, plongent, se relèvent. Ils sont très motivés.

Finalement, après un dernier échange impressionnant, un joueur marque le point final. La balle touche le sol. C'est fini ! Le gagnant lève les bras au ciel, très content. Son adversaire s'approche du filet, triste mais avec un bon esprit sportif. Ils se serrent la main.

Le public se lève et applaudit les deux joueurs. Quelle belle performance ! Quel match inoubliable ! Les spectateurs quittent le stade, encore surpris par ce qu'ils viennent de voir. Ce match restera sûrement dans les mémoires.

Explore the Translation

FS ▶ Un match de tennis passionnant

LT ▶ A match of tennis exciting

▼

NT ▶ An exciting tennis match

•••

FS ▶ Je suis au bord du terrain principal pour vous faire vivre ce match exceptionnel.

LT ▶ I am at the edge of the court main to you make live this match exceptional.

NT ▶ I am at the edge of the main court to bring you this exceptional match.

•••

FS ▶ L'ambiance est excitante !

LT ▶ The atmosphere is exciting!

NT ▶ The atmosphere is thrilling!

•••

FS ▶ Les spectateurs s'installent bruyamment dans les gradins.

LT ▶ The spectators themselves install noisily in the stands.

NT ▶ The spectators settle noisily into the stands.

•••

FS ▶ Vont-ils voir un match important ?

LT ▶ Will they see a match important?

▼

NT ▶ Will they see an important match?

•••

FS ▶ Les deux joueurs entrent sur le terrain.

LT ▶ The two players enter on the court.

▼

NT ▶ The two players step onto the court.

•••

FS ▶ Ils saluent le public qui les applaudit fort.

LT ▶ They greet the audience that them applauds strongly.

NT ▶ They greet the audience, which applauds them loudly.

•••

FS ▶ Chacun prend sa raquette et commence à s'échauffer.

LT ▶ Each one takes their racket and begins to themselves warm up.

NT ▶ Each one picks up their racket and begins to warm up.

•••

FS ▶ Ils frappent la balle avec force, se préparant pour le match à venir.

LT ▶ They hit the ball with force, themselves preparing for the match to come.

NT ▶ They hit the ball forcefully, preparing for the upcoming match.

•••

FS ▶ L'arbitre appelle les joueurs.

LT/NT ▶ The referee calls the players.

•••

FS ▶ Ils se placent de chaque côté du filet.

LT ▶ They themselves place on each side of the net.

NT ▶ They position themselves on either side of the net.

•••

FS ▶ Le premier service est lancé !

LT ▶ The first serve is launched!

NT ▶ The first serve is made!

•••

FS ▶ La balle passe au-dessus du filet très vite.

LT ▶ The ball passes over the net very quickly.

NT ▶ The ball flies over the net very quickly.

•••

FS ▶ Le receveur la renvoie avec difficulté.

LT ▶ The receiver it returns with difficulty.

▼

NT ▶ The receiver returns it with difficulty.

•••

FS ▶ Les échanges sont rapides et forts.

LT ▶ The exchanges are fast and strong.

▼

NT ▶ The rallies are fast and powerful.

•••

FS ▶ Les joueurs courent, glissent, frappent.
LT ▶ The players run, slide, hit.
▼
NT ▶ The players run, slide, and hit.

•••

FS ▶ Ils ne laissent rien passer.
LT ▶ They not let nothing pass.
▼
NT ▶ They don't let anything through.

•••

FS ▶ Le public ne fait pas de bruit.
LT ▶ The public makes not of noise.
▼
NT ▶ The audience remains silent.

•••

FS ▶ Chaque point est important.
LT ▶ Each point is important.
▼
NT ▶ Every point matters.

•••

FS ▶ Les spectateurs encouragent leurs favoris.
LT ▶ The spectators encourage their favorites.
▼
NT ▶ The spectators cheer for their favorites.

•••

FS ▶ "Allez !" crient-ils avec joie.
LT ▶ "Go!" shout they with joy.
▼
NT ▶ "Go!" they shout joyfully.

•••

FS ▶ L'ambiance est très bonne.

LT ▶ The atmosphere is very good.

▼

NT ▶ The atmosphere is fantastic.

•••

FS ▶ Un joueur marque un point superbe. La foule crie de joie !

LT ▶ A player scores a point superb. The crowd shouts with joy!

▼

NT ▶ A player scores a superb point. The crowd cheers with joy!

•••

FS ▶ Les applaudissements sont forts dans tout le stade.

LT ▶ The applauses are strong in all the stadium.

NT ▶ The applause is loud throughout the stadium.

•••

FS ▶ Le joueur lève le poing pour montrer sa joie.

LT ▶ The player raises the fist to show his joy.

NT ▶ The player raises his fist to show his joy.

•••

FS ▶ Son adversaire, lui, secoue la tête, triste.

LT ▶ His opponent, him, shakes the head, sad.

▼

NT ▶ His opponent shakes his head, looking sad.

•••

FS ▶ Mais le match n'est pas fini. Les jeux continuent.

LT ▶ But the match is not finished. The games continue.

▼

NT ▶ But the match isn't over. The games continue.

•••

FS ▶ Les joueurs ne semblent pas fatigués.

LT ▶ The players seem not tired.

▼

NT ▶ The players don't seem tired.

•••

FS ▶ Ils continuent à jouer avec la même force.

LT ▶ They continue to play with the same strength.

▼

NT ▶ They keep playing with the same intensity.

•••

FS ▶ Leurs coups sont précis et forts.

LT ▶ Their shots are precise and strong.

▼

NT ▶ Their shots are precise and powerful.

•••

FS ▶ La balle vole d'un côté à l'autre du terrain très vite.

LT ▶ The ball flies from one side to the other of the court very quickly.

▼

NT ▶ The ball flies quickly from one side of the court to the other.

•••

FS ▶ Soudain, un coup droit excellent !

LT ▶ Suddenly, a forehand excellent!

▼

NT ▶ Suddenly, an excellent forehand!

•••

FS ▶ La balle frôle la ligne. Est-elle dedans ou dehors ?

LT ▶ The ball grazes the line. Is it inside or outside?

▼

NT ▶ The ball barely touches the line. Is it in or out?

•••

FS ▶ L'arbitre annonce : "Dedans !".

LT ▶ The referee announces: "Inside!"

▼

NT ▶ The referee announces: "In!"

•••

FS ▶ Le point est bon. Quelle tension !

LT ▶ The point is good. What tension!

NT ▶ The point is valid. What suspense!

•••

FS ▶ Le match est serré. Aucun des joueurs ne veut perdre.

LT ▶ The match is tight. None of the players not wants to lose.

NT ▶ The match is close. Neither player wants to lose.

•••

FS ▶ Ils se battent pour chaque point.

LT ▶ They themselves fight for each point.

NT ▶ They fight for every point.

•••

FS ▶ Le public regarde sans bouger.

LT ▶ The public watches without moving.

NT ▶ The audience watches without moving.

***

FS ▶ Personne ne veut partir. Qui va gagner ?

LT ▶ Nobody not wants to leave. Who goes to win?

▼

NT ▶ No one wants to leave. Who will win?

***

FS ▶ Les échanges deviennent de plus en plus longs.

LT ▶ The exchanges become of more in more long.

▼

NT ▶ The rallies become longer and longer.

***

FS ▶ Les joueurs frappent la balle encore et encore.

LT ▶ The players hit the ball again and again.

NT ▶ The players hit the ball over and over.

***

FS ▶ Ils glissent, plongent, se relèvent. Ils sont très motivés.

LT ▶ They slide, dive, themselves get up again. They are very motivated.

NT ▶ They slide, dive, and get back up. They are highly motivated.

***

FS ▶ Finalement, après un dernier échange impressionnant, un joueur marque le point final.

LT ▶ Finally, after a last rally impressive, a player scores the point final.

NT ▶ Finally, after an impressive last rally, a player scores the final point.

***

FS ▶ La balle touche le sol. C'est fini !

LT ▶ The ball touches the ground. It is finished!

NT ▶ The ball hits the ground. It's over!

•••

FS ▶ Le gagnant lève les bras au ciel, très content.

LT ▶ The winner raises the arms to the sky, very happy.

NT ▶ The winner raises his arms to the sky, very happy.

•••

FS ▶ Son adversaire s'approche du filet, triste mais avec un bon esprit sportif.

LT ▶ His opponent himself approaches of the net, sad but with a good spirit sporting.

NT ▶ His opponent approaches the net, sad but with good sportsmanship.

•••

FS ▶ Ils se serrent la main.

LT ▶ They themselves shake the hand.

NT ▶ They shake hands.

•••

FS ▶ Le public se lève et applaudit les deux joueurs.

LT ▶ The public itself stands up and applauds the two players.

▼

NT ▶ The audience stands up and applauds both players.

•••

FS ▶ Quelle belle performance !

LT ▶ What beautiful performance!

NT ▶ What a great performance!

•••

FS ▶ Quel match inoubliable !

LT ▶ What match unforgettable!

NT ▶ What an unforgettable match!

•••

FS ▶ Les spectateurs quittent le stade, encore surpris par ce qu'ils viennent de voir.

LT ▶ The spectators leave the stadium, still surprised by what they come from to see.

NT ▶ The spectators leave the stadium, still amazed by what they have just seen.

•••

FS ▶ Ce match restera sûrement dans les mémoires.

LT ▶ This match will remain surely in the memories.

NT ▶ This match will surely remain in their memories.

•••

Put Your Learning to the Test

1. Translate the following sentences using the vocabulary from the story:

a) Les spectateurs s'installent dans les gradins avant le match.

____

b) L'arbitre annonce le début du match et les joueurs se placent sur le terrain.

____

c) Le public applaudit quand un joueur marque un point.

____

d) Après un long échange, un joueur gagne le dernier point et célèbre sa victoire.

____

2. Rearrange the order of the following words to form a correct sentence:

a) installent gradins spectateurs Les s' dans les

____

b) d'un balle La terrain vole l'autre côté à

____

c) est très serré et difficile match Ce

____

d) gagnant Le ciel bras lève les au

____

3. Translate the following words from French to English:

a) court ___________ d) racket ___________

b) referee ___________ e) stands ___________

c) net ___________ f) applause ___________

4. Why is the match so exciting for the spectators?

a) Because they are playing in complete silence.

b) Because the players are very strong and fight for every point.

c) Because the players make many mistakes.

d) Because the referee keeps stopping the match.

5. Determine if the following statements are true or false:

a) _______ The referee starts the match by serving the ball.

b) _______ The spectators are silent throughout the match.

c) _______ The players continue to play with a lot of energy.

d) _______ The losing player leaves the court without greeting his opponent.

Review your answers on the next page.

Answer Key

1. a) The spectators settle into the stands before the match.

   b) The referee announces the start of the match, and the players take their positions on the court.

   c) The crowd applauds when a player scores a point.

   d) After a long rally, a player wins the final point and celebrates his victory.

2. a) Les spectateurs s'installent dans les gradins.

   b) La balle vole d'un côté à l'autre du terrain.

   c) Ce match est très serré et difficile.

   d) Le gagnant lève les bras au ciel.

3. a) terrain b) arbitre c) filet

   d) raquette e) gradins f) applaudissements

4. b) Because the players are very strong and fight for every point.

5. a) False b) False c) True d) False

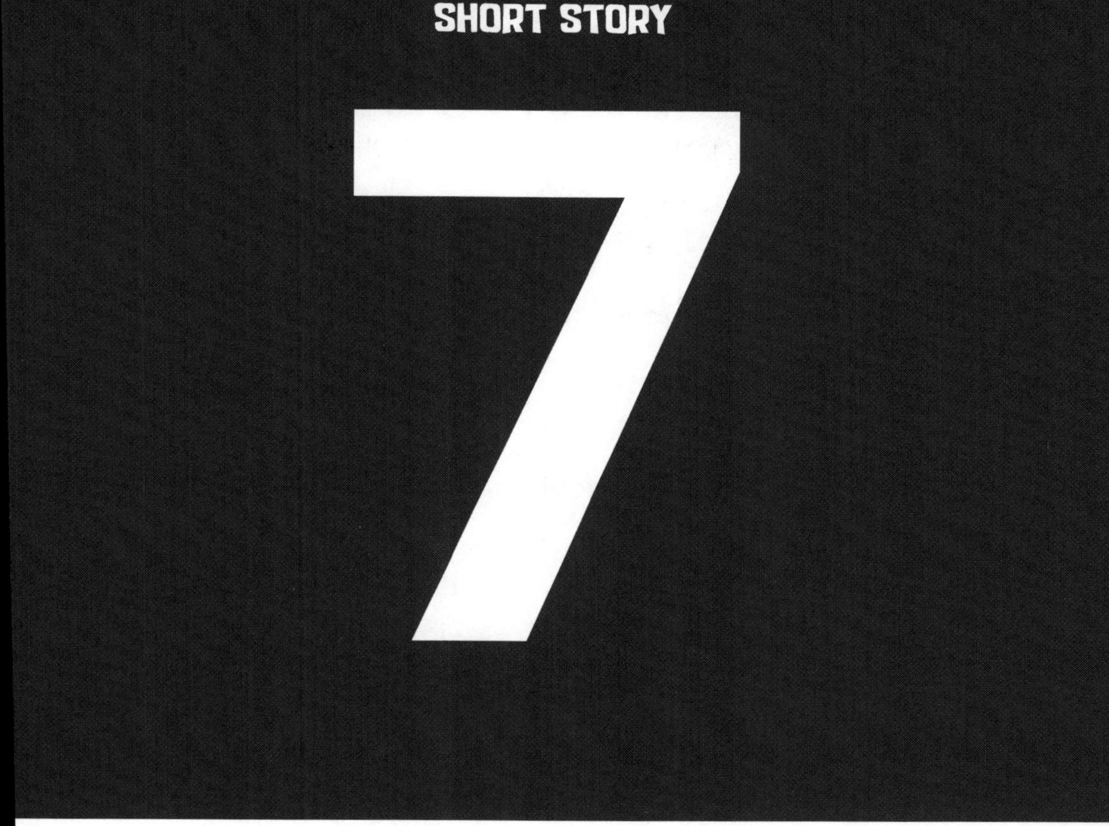

Main verb tense:
Present simple
(Présent de l'indicatif)

Main persons:
1st and 2nd person plural
(1ère et 2ème personne du pluriel)

Text type:
Dialogue and narrative
(Dialogue et récit)

Vocabulary theme:
Restaurant dining
(Le repas au restaurant)

Listening to the story is key to mastering pronunciation and an essential step in your learning journey.

- Start with **slow audio** if you need extra clarity.
- Listen at **normal speed** to get used to natural French.
- Challenge yourself with **fast audio** when you're ready.
- **Practice pronunciation:** Pause after each sentence and repeat it out loud!

Find the audio download on page 12.

Un repas au restaurant

Ce samedi soir, nous allons dîner au restaurant avec notre couple d'amis, les Girard.

Nous entrons dans le restaurant et le serveur nous accueille avec un sourire.

Serveur : Bonsoir, avez-vous une réservation ?

M. Martin : Oui, nous avons réservé une table pour quatre personnes au nom de Martin.

Serveur : Parfait, suivez-moi s'il vous plaît. Voici votre table.

Nous nous asseyons et le serveur nous donne les menus.

Serveur : Voici la carte. Désirez-vous un apéritif pour commencer ?

Mme Girard : Oui, nous prendrons quatre verres de vin blanc, s'il vous plaît.

Pendant que nous attendons nos apéritifs, nous regardons le menu.

M. Martin : Que pensez-vous prendre comme entrée ?

Mme Girard : Nous hésitons entre la salade verte et le pâté de campagne. Et vous ?

M. Martin : Nous allons essayer la soupe à l'oignon gratinée. C'est une spécialité du restaurant.

Le serveur revient avec nos apéritifs.

Serveur : Voici vos verres de vin blanc. Êtes-vous prêts à commander ?

Mme Girard : Oui, nous sommes prêts. Pour l'entrée, nous prendrons deux salades vertes.

M. Martin : Et pour nous, ce sera deux soupes à l'oignon gratinées, s'il vous plaît.

Serveur : Très bien, et pour le plat principal ?

M. Girard : Nous aimerions le steak frites pour deux personnes.

Serveur : Parfait. Comment voulez-vous la cuisson de vos steaks ?

Mme Girard : À point pour moi, s'il vous plaît.

M. Girard : Et saignant pour moi.

Mme Martin : Et nous, nous choisirons le poisson du jour avec des légumes de saison.

Serveur : Excellent choix. Désirez-vous du vin rouge avec votre repas ?

M. Girard : Oui, pouvez-vous nous recommander un bon vin rouge ?

Serveur : Bien sûr, nous avons un excellent Bordeaux qui se marie bien avec le steak.

M. Martin : Parfait, nous prendrons une bouteille pour la table.

Le repas se déroule dans une ambiance agréable. Nous discutons et rions ensemble.

Après le plat principal, le serveur revient.

Serveur : Avez-vous encore de la place pour un dessert ?

Mme Martin : Oui, nous aimerions voir la carte des desserts, s'il vous plaît.

Mme Girard : Oh, le gâteau au chocolat a l'air délicieux !

M. Martin : Nous, nous penchons plutôt pour la tarte aux pommes. Que choisissez-vous finalement ?

M. Girard : Nous allons prendre deux gâteaux au chocolat.

Mme Martin : Et pour nous, ce sera deux tartes aux pommes.

À la fin du repas, nous sommes tous satisfaits.

Serveur : Avez-vous apprécié votre repas ?

M. Martin : Oui, c'était excellent. Pouvons-nous avoir l'addition, s'il vous plaît ?

Mme Girard : Le repas était vraiment délicieux. Nous reviendrons certainement !

Nous payons l'addition et quittons le restaurant, heureux d'avoir partagé ce bon moment entre amis.

Explore the Translation

FS ▶ Un repas au restaurant

LT ▶ A meal at the restaurant

NT ▶ A meal at a restaurant

•••

FS ▶ Ce samedi soir, nous allons dîner au restaurant avec notre couple d'amis, les Girard.

LT ▶ This Saturday evening, we go to dine at restaurant with our couple of friends, the Girard.

NT ▶ This Saturday evening, we're dining out with our couple of friends, the Girards.

•••

FS ▶ Nous entrons dans le restaurant et le serveur nous accueille avec un sourire.

LT ▶ We enter in the restaurant and the waiter us welcomes with a smile.

NT ▶ We walk into the restaurant, and the waiter greets us with a smile.

•••

FS ▶ Serveur : Bonsoir, avez-vous une réservation ?

LT ▶ Good evening, have you a reservation?

NT ▶ Good evening, do you have a reservation?

•••

FS ▶ M. Martin : Oui, nous avons réservé une table pour quatre personnes au nom de Martin.

LT ▶ Yes, we have reserved a table for four persons at name of Martin.

▼

NT ▶ Yes, we booked a table for four under the name Martin.

•••

FS ▶ Serveur : Parfait, suivez-moi s'il vous plaît. Voici votre table.

LT ▶ Perfect, follow me if it you pleases. Here is your table.

NT ▶ Great, please follow me. Here's your table.

•••

FS ▶ Nous nous asseyons et le serveur nous donne les menus.

LT ▶ We ourselves sit and the waiter us gives the menus.

NT ▶ We sit down and the waiter gives us the menus.

•••

FS ▶ Serveur : Voici la carte. Désirez-vous un apéritif pour commencer ?

LT ▶ Here is the card. Desire you an aperitif to begin?

NT ▶ Here's the menu. Would you like a drink to start?

•••

FS ▶ Mme Girard : Oui, nous prendrons quatre verres de vin blanc, s'il vous plaît.

LT ▶ Yes, we will take four glasses of wine white, if it you pleases.

NT ▶ Yes, we'll have four glasses of white wine, please.

•••

FS ▶ Pendant que nous attendons nos apéritifs, nous regardons le menu.

LT ▶ During that we wait our aperitifs, we look the menu.

▼

NT ▶ While we wait for our drinks, we look at the menu.

•••

FS ▶ M. Martin : Que pensez-vous prendre comme entrée ?

LT ▶ What think you take as appetizer?

▼

NT ▶ What are you thinking of having for appetizer?

•••

FS ▶ Mme Girard : Nous hésitons entre la salade verte et le pâté de campagne. Et vous ?

LT ▶ We hesitate between the salad green and the pâté of countryside. And you?

NT ▶ We're torn between the green salad and the country pâté. How about you?

•••

FS ▶ M. Martin : Nous allons essayer la soupe à l'oignon gratinée.

LT ▶ We go to try the soup with onion gratinated.

NT ▶ We're going to try the French onion soup au gratin.

•••

FS ▶ C'est une spécialité du restaurant.

LT ▶ It is a specialty of the restaurant.

NT ▶ It's a restaurant specialty.

•••

FS ▶ Le serveur revient avec nos apéritifs.

LT ▶ The waiter returns with our aperitifs.

▼

NT ▶ The waiter returns with our drinks.

•••

FS ▶ Serveur : Voici vos verres de vin blanc.

LT/ NT ▶ Here are your glasses of wine white.

•••

FS ▶ Serveur : Êtes-vous prêts à commander ?

LT/ NT ▶ Are you ready to order?

•••

FS ▶ Mme Girard : Oui, nous sommes prêts. Pour l'entrée, nous prendrons deux salades vertes.

LT ▶ Yes, we are ready. For the appetizer, we will take two salads green.

NT ▶ Yes, we're ready. For appetizers, we'll have two salads.

•••

FS ▶ M. Martin : Et pour nous, ce sera deux soupes à l'oignon gratinées, s'il vous plaît.

LT ▶ And for us, it will be two soups with onion gratinated, if it you pleases.

NT ▶ And for us, two onion soups au gratin, please.

•••

FS ▶ Serveur : Très bien, et pour le plat principal ?

LT ▶ Very well, and for the dish main?

NT ▶ Very well, and for the main course?

•••

FS ▶ M. Girard : Nous aimerions le steak frites pour deux personnes.

LT ▶ We would like the steak fries for two persons.

NT ▶ We'd like steak and French fries for two.

•••

FS ▶ Serveur : Parfait. Comment voulez-vous la cuisson de vos steaks ?

LT ▶ Perfect. How want you the cooking of your steaks?

NT ▶ Perfect. How would you like your steaks cooked?

•••

FS ▶ Mme Girard : À point pour moi, s'il vous plaît.

LT ▶ To point for me, if it you pleases.

NT ▶ Medium for me, please.

•••

FS ▶ M. Girard : Et saignant pour moi.

LT ▶ And bleeding for me.

NT ▶ And rare for me.

•••

FS ▶ Mme Martin : Et nous, nous choisirons le poisson du jour avec des légumes de saison.

LT ▶ And us, we will choose the fish of the day with some vegetables of season.

NT ▶ And we'll choose the fish of the day with seasonal vegetables.

•••

FS ▶ Serveur : Excellent choix. Désirez-vous du vin rouge avec votre repas ?

LT ▶ Excellent choice. Desire you some wine red with your meal?

NT ▶ Excellent choice. Would you like some red wine with your meal?

•••

FS ▶ M. Girard : Oui, pouvez-vous nous recommander un bon vin rouge ?

LT ▶ Yes, can you us recommend a good wine red?

NT ▶ Yes, can you recommend a good red wine?

•••

FS ▶ Serveur : Bien sûr, nous avons un excellent Bordeaux qui se marie bien avec le steak.

LT ▶ Well sure, we have an excellent Bordeaux which itself marries well with the steak.

NT ▶ Of course, we have an excellent Bordeaux that goes well with steak.

•••

FS ▶ M. Martin : Parfait, nous prendrons une bouteille pour la table.

LT ▶ Perfect, we will take a bottle for the table.

NT ▶ Perfect, we'll take a bottle for the table.

•••

FS ▶ Le repas se déroule dans une ambiance agréable. Nous discutons et rions ensemble.

LT ▶ The meal itself unfolds in an atmosphere pleasant. We discuss and laugh together.

NT ▶ The meal is going well, and we're chatting and laughing

together.

•••

FS ▶ Après le plat principal, le serveur revient.

LT ▶ After the dish main, the waiter returns.

▼

NT ▶ After the main course, the waiter returns.

•••

FS ▶ Serveur : Avez-vous encore de la place pour un dessert ?

LT ▶ Have you still of the place for a dessert?

NT ▶ Do you still have room for dessert?

•••

FS ▶ Mme Martin : Oui, nous aimerions voir la carte des desserts, s'il vous plaît.

LT ▶ Yes, we would like to see the menu of the desserts, if it you pleases.

NT ▶ Yes, we'd like to see the dessert menu, please.

•••

FS ▶ Mme Girard : Oh, le gâteau au chocolat a l'air délicieux !

LT ▶ Oh, the cake with chocolate has the air delicious!

NT ▶ Oh, the chocolate cake looks delicious!

•••

FS ▶ M. Martin : Nous, nous penchons plutôt pour la tarte aux pommes.

LT ▶ Us, we lean rather for the pie with apples.

NT ▶ We're leaning towards the apple pie.

•••

FS ▶ M. Martin : Que choisissez-vous finalement ?

LT ▶ What choose you finally?

NT ▶ What's your final choice?

•••

FS ▶ M. Girard : Nous allons prendre deux gâteaux au chocolat.

LT ▶ We go to take two cakes with chocolate.

NT ▶ We'll have two chocolate cakes.

•••

FS ▶ Mme Martin : Et pour nous, ce sera deux tartes aux pommes.

LT ▶ And for us, it will be two tarts with apples.

NT ▶ And for us, two apple pies.

•••

FS ▶ À la fin du repas, nous sommes tous satisfaits.

LT ▶ At the end of the meal, we are all satisfied.

NT ▶ At the end of the meal, we're all satisfied.

•••

FS ▶ Serveur : Avez-vous apprécié votre repas ?

LT ▶ Have you appreciated your meal?

NT ▶ Did you enjoy your meal?

•••

FS ▶ M. Martin : Oui, c'était excellent.

LT ▶ Yes, it was excellent.

▼

NT ▶ Yes, it was excellent.

•••

FS ▶ M. Martin : Pouvons-nous avoir l'addition, s'il vous plaît ?

LT ▶ Can we have the bill, if it you pleases?

NT ▶ Can we have the bill, please?

•••

FS ▶ Mme Girard : Le repas était vraiment délicieux.

LT ▶ The meal was truly delicious.

▼

NT ▶ The meal was really delicious.

•••

FS ▶ Mme Girard : Nous reviendrons certainement !

LT ▶ We will return certainly!

NT ▶ We'll definitely be back!

•••

FS ▶ Nous payons l'addition et quittons le restaurant, heureux d'avoir partagé ce bon moment entre amis.

LT ▶ We pay the bill and leave the restaurant, happy to have shared this good moment between friends.

NT ▶ We pay the check and leave the restaurant, happy to have shared this good time with friends.

•••

Put Your Learning to the Test

1. Translate the following sentences using the vocabulary from the story:

a) Nous avons réservé une table pour quatre personnes.

____

b) Le serveur nous apporte la carte et nous prenons un apéritif.

____

c) Nous hésitons entre la soupe à l'oignon et la salade verte.

____

d) À la fin du repas, nous demandons l'addition et quittons le restaurant.

____

2. Rearrange the order of the following words to form a correct sentence:

a) sourire avec un accueille serveur nous Le

____

b) Nous restaurant quittons contents le du repas

____

c) entrée Que prendre vous comme pensez-?

____

d) tarte à chocolat le préfère au gâteau Je la

____

3. Translate the following words from French to English:

a) serveur __________ d) plat principal __________

b) entrée __________ e) dessert __________

c) repas __________ f) addition __________

4. Circle the odd one out:

a) commander - addition - manger - choisir

b) soupe - salade - steak - gâteau

c) serveur - excellent - délicieux - agréable

d) serveur - client - cuisinier - vin

5. Why does M. Martin order a Bordeaux?

a) Because it is the cheapest wine on the menu.

b) Because it pairs well with the steak.

c) Because Mme Martin asked for it.

d) Because the waiter suggested it with the dessert

6. Determine if the following statements are true or false:

a) ______ The group orders four glasses of red wine as an aperitif.

b) ______ M. Girard prefers his steak well-done.

c) ______ The group orders two different types of desserts.

d) ______ At the end of the meal, they decide never to return to the restaurant.

Review your answers on the next page.

Answer Key

1. a) We reserved a table for four people.

   b) The waiter brings us the menu, and we order an aperitif.

   c) We hesitate between the onion soup and the green salad.

   d) At the end of the meal, we ask for the bill and leave the restaurant.

2. a) Le serveur nous accueille avec un sourire.

   b) Nous quittons le restaurant contents du repas.

   c) Que pensez-vous prendre comme entrée ?

   d) Je préfère le gâteau au chocolat à la tarte.

3. a) waiter b) appetizer c) meal

   d) main course e) dessert f) bill

4. a) addition
   The others are verbs related to ordering food, but "addition" is the bill.

   b) gâteau
   The others are main courses or appetizers, but "gâteau" is a dessert.

   c) serveur
   The others are adjectives describing the meal or atmosphere, but "serveur" is a person.

   d) vin
   The others are people in a restaurant, but "vin" is a drink.

5. b) Because it pairs well with the steak.

6. a) False b) False c) True d) False

Main verb tenses:
Imperative and Present simple
(Impératif et Présent de l'indicatif)

Main persons:
2nd person singular and plural, 3rd person singular
(2e personne du singulier et du pluriel, 3e personne du singulier)

Text type:
Dialogue and narration
(Dialogue et narration)

Vocabulary theme:
Cooking
(La cuisine)

Listening to the story is key to mastering pronunciation and an essential step in your learning journey.

- Start with **slow audio** if you need extra clarity.
- Listen at **normal speed** to get used to natural French.
- Challenge yourself with **fast audio** when you're ready.
- **Practice pronunciation:** Pause after each sentence and repeat it out loud!

Find the audio download on page 12.

Une leçon de cuisine en famille

Aujourd'hui, tu apprends à faire la tarte aux pommes familiale. Vous êtes dans la cuisine, ta mère et toi. À 35 ans, tu décides enfin d'apprendre cette recette traditionnelle.

"D'abord, lave les pommes," dit ta mère. Tu les laves soigneusement.

"Maintenant, épluche-les," continue-t-elle. Tu prends l'éplucheur et tu commences.

Pendant ce temps, ta mère prépare la pâte. Elle mélange la farine, le beurre et l'eau.

"Observe bien mes gestes," dit-elle. "La consistance est cruciale."

Tu regardes attentivement, notant chaque étape. Ta mère ajoute une pincée de sel.

"À toi maintenant," dit-elle. "Pétris la pâte avec tes mains."

Tu plonges tes mains dans la pâte, surpris par la texture.

"Ajoute un peu de farine si c'est trop collant," conseille ta mère.

Elle coupe les pommes en tranches fines. "L'épaisseur influence la cuisson," explique-t-elle.

"Étale la pâte dans le moule," demande ta mère. Tu utilises le rouleau à pâtisserie.

"Bien. Maintenant, dispose les pommes sur la pâte."

Tu arranges soigneusement les tranches, créant un motif circulaire.

Ta mère prépare un mélange de sucre et de cannelle. "Saupoudre-le sur les pommes," indique-t-elle.

Tu saupoudres le mélange avec précision.

"Parfait. On va la mettre au four," dit ta mère.

Pendant la cuisson, vous nettoyez la cuisine. L'odeur familière se répand dans la maison.

"Cette recette se transmet depuis des générations," dit ta mère.

Quand le minuteur sonne, ta mère sort la tarte. Elle est parfaitement dorée.

"Félicitations pour ta première tarte aux pommes familiale," dit-elle.

À ce moment, le reste de la famille arrive pour le goûter.

"Allons leur montrer," dit ta mère. "Apporte la tarte."

Dans la salle à manger, ta mère annonce : "Regardez la magnifique tarte que nous avons faite !"

Les compliments fusent. Tu poses la tarte au centre de la table, satisfait.

"Elle a l'air délicieuse," dit ton père.

Ta mère sourit et dit : "C'est une réalisation à quatre mains. Servez-vous et dites-nous ce que vous en pensez !"

Pendant que tous dégustent, tu échanges un regard complice avec ta mère. Cette leçon restera un moment précieux, marquant la transmission d'un héritage familial.

Explore the Translation

FS ▶ Une leçon de cuisine en famille

LT ▶ A lesson of cooking in family

NT ▶ A family cooking lesson

•••

FS ▶ Aujourd'hui, tu apprends à faire la tarte aux pommes familiale.

LT ▶ Today, you learn to make the pie of apples familial.

NT ▶ Today, you're learning how to make the family apple pie.

•••

FS ▶ Vous êtes dans la cuisine, ta mère et toi.
LT ▶ You are in the kitchen, your mother and you.
▼
NT ▶ You and your mother are in the kitchen.

•••

FS ▶ À 35 ans, tu décides enfin d'apprendre cette recette traditionnelle.
LT ▶ At 35 years, you decide finally to learn this recipe traditional.
▼
NT ▶ At 35, you finally decide to learn this traditional recipe.

•••

FS ▶ "D'abord, lave les pommes," dit ta mère.
LT/NT ▶ "First, wash the apples," says your mother.

•••

FS ▶ Tu les laves soigneusement. "Maintenant, épluche-les," continue-t-elle.
LT ▶ You them wash carefully. "Now, peel them," continues she.
▼
NT ▶ You wash them carefully. "Now peel them," she continues.

•••

FS ▶ Tu prends l'éplucheur et tu commences.
LT ▶ You take the peeler and you begin.
▼
NT ▶ You take the peeler and start.

•••

FS ▶ Pendant ce temps, ta mère prépare la pâte.

LT ▶ During this time, your mother prepares the dough.

NT ▶ Meanwhile, your mother is preparing the dough.

•••

FS ▶ Elle mélange la farine, le beurre et l'eau.

LT ▶ She mixes the flour, the butter and the water.

NT ▶ She mixes flour, butter and water.

•••

FS ▶ "Observe bien mes gestes," dit-elle. "La consistance est cruciale."

LT ▶ "Observe well my gestures," says she. "The consistency is crucial."

NT ▶ "Watch me carefully," she says. Consistency is the key."

•••

FS ▶ Tu regardes attentivement, notant chaque étape.

LT ▶ You watch attentively, noting each step.

NT ▶ You watch carefully, taking note of each step.

•••

FS ▶ Ta mère ajoute une pincée de sel.

LT/NT ▶ Your mother adds a pinch of salt.

•••

FS ▶ "À toi maintenant," dit-elle. "Pétris la pâte avec tes mains."

LT ▶ "To you now," says she. "Knead the dough with your hands."

NT ▶ "Now it's your turn," she says. "Knead the dough with your hands."

•••

FS ▶ Tu plonges tes mains dans la pâte, surpris par la texture.

LT ▶ You plunge your hands in the dough, surprised by the texture.

▼

NT ▶ You plunge your hands into the dough, surprised by the texture.

•••

FS ▶ "Ajoute un peu de farine si c'est trop collant," conseille ta mère.

LT ▶ "Add a little of flour if it's too sticky," advises your mother.

▼

NT ▶ "Add a little flour if it's too sticky," advises your mother.

•••

FS ▶ Elle coupe les pommes en tranches fines.

LT ▶ She cuts the apples in slices thin.

NT ▶ She cuts the apples into thin slices.

•••

FS ▶ "L'épaisseur influence la cuisson," explique-t-elle.

LT ▶ "The thickness influences the cooking," explains she.

NT ▶ "Thickness affects cooking," she explains.

•••

FS ▶ "Étale la pâte dans le moule," demande ta mère.

LT ▶ "Spread the dough in the pan," asks your mother.

NT ▶ "Spread the pastry in the pan," your mother asks.

•••

FS ▶ Tu utilises le rouleau à pâtisserie.

LT ▶ You use the roll to pastry.

NT ▶ You use the rolling pin.

•••

FS ▶ "Bien. Maintenant, dispose les pommes sur la pâte."

LT ▶ "Good. Now, arrange the apples on the dough."

NT ▶ " Great. Now, lay the apples on the dough."

•••

FS ▶ Tu arranges soigneusement les tranches, créant un motif circulaire.

LT ▶ You arrange carefully the slices, creating a pattern circular.

NT ▶ You arrange the slices carefully in a circular pattern.

•••

FS ▶ Ta mère prépare un mélange de sucre et de cannelle.

LT ▶ Your mother prepares a mixture of sugar and of cinnamon.

NT ▶ Your mother prepares a mixture of sugar and cinnamon.

•••

FS ▶ "Saupoudre-le sur les pommes," indique-t-elle.

LT ▶ "Sprinkle it on the apples," indicates she.

▼

NT ▶ "Sprinkle it over the apples," she says.

•••

FS ▶ Tu saupoudres le mélange avec précision.

LT/NT ▶ You sprinkle the mixture with precision.

•••

FS ▶ "Parfait. On va la mettre au four," dit ta mère.

LT ▶ "Perfect. We will it put in oven," says your mother.

NT ▶ "Perfect. We'll put it in the oven," says your mother.

•••

FS ▶ Pendant la cuisson, vous nettoyez la cuisine.

LT ▶ During the cooking, you clean the kitchen.

▼

NT ▶ While it bakes, you clean the kitchen.

•••

FS ▶ L'odeur familière se répand dans la maison.

LT ▶ The smell familiar itself spreads in the house.

NT ▶ The familiar smell spreads through the house.

•••

FS ▶ "Cette recette se transmet depuis des générations," dit ta mère.

LT ▶ "This recipe itself transmits since some generations," says your mother.

NT ▶ "This recipe has been passed down for generations," says your mother.

•••

FS ▶ Quand le minuteur sonne, ta mère sort la tarte.

LT ▶ When the timer rings, your mother takes out the pie.

NT ▶ When the timer goes off, your mother takes out the pie.

•••

FS ▶ Elle est parfaitement dorée.

LT/NT ▶ It is perfectly golden.

•••

FS ▶ "Félicitations pour ta première tarte aux pommes familiale," dit-elle.

LT ▶ "Congratulations for your first pie to apples familial," says she.

NT ▶ "Congratulations on your first family apple pie," she says.

•••

FS ▶ À ce moment, le reste de la famille arrive pour le goûter.

LT ▶ At this moment, the rest of the family arrives for the snack.

NT ▶ Just then, the rest of the family arrives for the snack.

•••

FS ▶ "Allons leur montrer," dit ta mère. "Apporte la tarte."

LT ▶ "Let's go to them show," says your mother. "Bring the pie.

NT ▶ "Let's show them," says your mother. "Bring the pie.

•••

FS ▶ Dans la salle à manger, ta mère annonce : "Regardez la magnifique tarte que nous avons faite !"

LT ▶ In the room to eating, your mother announces: "Look at the magnificent pie that we have made!"

NT ▶ In the dining room, your mother announces, "Look at the wonderful pie we've made!"

•••

FS ▶ Les compliments fusent. Tu poses la tarte au centre de la table, satisfait.

LT ▶ The compliments burst. You place the pie at center of the table, satisfied.

NT ▶ The compliments pour in. You set the pie in the middle of the table, feeling proud.

***

FS ▶ "Elle a l'air délicieuse," dit ton père.

LT ▶ "It has the air delicious," says your father.

▼

NT ▶ "It looks delicious," says your father.

***

FS ▶ Ta mère sourit et dit : "C'est une réalisation à quatre mains."

LT ▶ Your mother smiles and says: "It is a realization at four hands."

▼

NT ▶ Your mother smiles and says, "This is a four-hands creation."

***

FS ▶ "Servez-vous et dites-nous ce que vous en pensez !"

LT ▶ "Serve yourselves and tell us what you of it think!"

▼

NT ▶ "Help yourselves and tell us what you think!"

***

FS ▶ Pendant que tous dégustent, tu échanges un regard complice avec ta mère.

LT ▶ While that all taste, you exchange a look complicit with your mother.

▼

NT ▶ As everyone enjoys the pie, you share a knowing glance with your mother.

***

FS ▶ Cette leçon restera un moment précieux, marquant la transmission d'un héritage familial.

LT ▶ This lesson will remain a moment precious, marking the transmission of a heritage familial.

▼

NT ▶ This lesson will remain a precious moment, marking the passing on of a family heritage.

Put Your Learning to the Test

1. Translate the following sentences using the vocabulary from the story:

    a) Ma mère mélange la farine, le beurre et l'eau pour préparer la pâte.

    ____

    b) J'épluche les pommes et les coupe en fines tranches.

    ____

    c) Nous saupoudrons du sucre et de la cannelle sur la tarte.

    ____

    d) L'odeur de la tarte aux pommes se répand dans la maison pendant la cuisson.

    ____

2. Rearrange the order of the following words to form a correct sentence:

    a) prends Tu et commences éplucheur l' tu

    ____

    b) pommes fines coupe en les tranches Elle

    ____

    c) mains les Il avec la pâte bien faut pétrir

    ____

    d) famille le pour Le goûter arrive reste la de

    ____

3. Translate the following words from French to English:

a) farine ____________ d) moule ____________

b) pâte ____________ e) cuisson ____________

c) couteau ____________ f) cannelle ____________

4. Complete the sentences with the correct word from the list:

Words: pâte, pommes, four, sucre

Use each word only once

a) Nous lavons, épluchons et coupons les ______________ avant de les disposer dans le moule.

b) Ma mère prépare la ______________ en mélangeant de la farine, du beurre et de l'eau.

c) Nous mettons la tarte au ______________ pour la cuisson.

d) Nous saupoudrons du ______________ et de la cannelle sur les fruits.

5. Determine if the following statements are true or false:

a) _______ The mother prepares the dough while the other person washes the apples.

b) _______ The apples are cut before being peeled.

c) _______ The thickness of the apple slices affects the baking process.

d) _______ The father is the one who suggests adding cinnamon to the recipe.

Review your answers on the next page.

Answer Key

1. a) My mother mixes the flour, butter, and water to prepare the dough.

   b) I peel the apples and cut them into thin slices.

   c) We sprinkle sugar and cinnamon on the tart.

   d) The smell of apple tart spreads through the house while it bakes.

2. a) Tu prends l'éplucheur et tu commences.

   b) Elle coupe les pommes en fines tranches.

   c) Il faut bien pétrir la pâte avec les mains.

   d) Le reste de la famille arrive pour le goûter.

3. a) flour   b) dough   c) knife

   d) baking dish   e) baking   f) cinnamon

4. a) pommes   b) pâte   c) four   d) sucre

5. a) True   b) False   c) True   d) False

Main verb tense:
Near future
(Futur proche)

Main persons:
1st person singular and 3rd person singular
(1ère personne du singulier et 3e personne du singulier)

Text type:
Descriptive narrative
(Récit descriptif)

Vocabulary theme:
City, public places, directions, transportation
(Ville, lieux publics, directions, transports)

Listening to the story is key to mastering pronunciation and an essential step in your learning journey.

- Start with **slow audio** if you need extra clarity.
- Listen at **normal speed** to get used to natural French.
- Challenge yourself with **fast audio** when you're ready.
- **Practice pronunciation:** Pause after each sentence and repeat it out loud!

Find the audio download on page 12.

Une promenade en ville

Demain, je vais explorer le centre-ville. Je me demande quelles surprises cette journée me réservera.

Je vais commencer ma promenade tôt le matin, quand la ville va tout juste s'éveiller. Le boulanger va ouvrir sa boutique, et l'odeur du pain frais va embaumer la rue. Vais-je résister à la tentation d'acheter un croissant encore chaud ?

À 9h, je vais me diriger vers la place principale. La fontaine au centre va déjà être en marche, ses jets d'eau scintillant au soleil matinal.

Les pigeons vont se rassembler autour, cherchant quelques miettes. Un vieil homme va probablement être là, comme chaque jour, pour les nourrir. Va-t-il me raconter une de ses histoires si je m'approche ?

Ensuite, je vais emprunter la rue commerçante. Les boutiques vont ouvrir leurs portes une à une. Les vendeurs vont installer leurs étalages colorés de fruits et légumes sur le trottoir.

Je vais peut-être acheter quelques fruits frais pour mon casse-croûte de midi. Le fleuriste du coin va arranger ses bouquets devant sa devanture. Ses fleurs vont apporter une touche de couleur à la rue grise.

Vers midi, je vais me rendre au parc municipal. Il va être rempli de familles et de personnes qui font leur jogging, profitant du beau temps.

Les enfants vont jouer sur les balançoires et le toboggan. Un couple va pique-niquer sur l'herbe verte. Vais-je trouver un banc libre pour manger mon casse-croûte ?

Dans l'après-midi, je vais visiter le musée d'art moderne. Une nouvelle exposition va ouvrir ses portes. Les œuvres vont sûrement être intéressantes, mais vais-je tout comprendre ? Le guide va certainement pouvoir m'expliquer les pièces les plus difficiles.

Pour terminer ma journée, je vais prendre le tramway jusqu'au vieux quartier. Les rues pavées vont être animées par les terrasses des cafés.

Les musiciens de rue vont jouer leurs mélodies entraînantes. Le soleil couchant va dorer les façades des vieilles maisons. Quel restaurant vais-je choisir pour dîner ? Il y en a tellement !

En rentrant, je vais passer par le pont qui passe au-dessus de la rivière. Les lumières de la ville vont se refléter dans l'eau, créant un spectacle magique.

Un bateau-mouche va glisser silencieusement sous le pont, transportant des touristes émerveillés.

Cette journée promet d'être riche en découvertes et en rencontres. La ville va dévoiler ses secrets au fil de mes pas.

Quels souvenirs vais-je garder de cette promenade ? Une chose est sûre, je vais voir ma ville d'un œil nouveau.

Explore the Translation

FS ▶ Une promenade en ville

LT/NT ▶ A walk in town

•••

FS ▶ Demain, je vais explorer le centre-ville.

LT ▶ Tomorrow, I go to explore the center city.

NT ▶ Tomorrow I'm going to explore downtown.

•••

FS ▶ Je me demande quelles surprises cette journée me réservera.

LT ▶ I myself ask which surprises this day to me will reserve.

NT ▶ I wonder what surprises the day will bring.

•••

FS ▶ Je vais commencer ma promenade tôt le matin, quand la ville va tout juste s'éveiller.

LT ▶ I go to begin my walk early the morning, when the city goes all just itself wake.

▼

NT ▶ I'll start my walk early, when the city is just beginning to wake up.

•••

FS ▶ Le boulanger va ouvrir sa boutique, et l'odeur du pain frais va embaumer la rue.

LT ▶ The baker goes open his shop, and the smell of the bread fresh goes perfume the street.

▼

NT ▶ The baker will open his store, and the smell of fresh bread will fill the street.

•••

FS ▶ Vais-je résister à la tentation d'acheter un croissant encore chaud ?

LT ▶ Go I to resist to the temptation of to buy a croissant still hot?

▼

NT ▶ Will I resist the temptation to buy a croissant while it's still warm?

•••

FS ▶ À 9h, je vais me diriger vers la place principale.

LT ▶ At 9 a.m., I go myself to direct towards the place main.

NT ▶ At 9 a.m., I'll head for the main square.

•••

FS ▶ La fontaine au centre va déjà être en marche, ses jets d'eau scintillant au soleil matinal.

LT ▶ The fountain at the center goes already to be running, its jets of water sparkling at the sun morning.

NT ▶ The fountain in the center will already be running, its water jets

sparkling in the morning sun.

•••

FS ▶ Les pigeons vont se rassembler autour, cherchant quelques miettes.

LT ▶ The pigeons go themselves to gather around, searching some crumbs.

NT ▶ The pigeons will gather around it, looking for a few crumbs.

•••

FS ▶ Un vieil homme va probablement être là, comme chaque jour, pour les nourrir.

LT ▶ An old man goes probably to be there, like each day, for them feed.

NT ▶ An old man will probably be there, as he is every day, to feed them.

•••

FS ▶ Va-t-il me raconter une de ses histoires si je m'approche ?

LT ▶ Goes he me to tell one of his stories if I myself approach?

NT ▶ Will he tell me one of his stories if I approach?

•••

FS ▶ Ensuite, je vais emprunter la rue commerçante.

LT ▶ Next, I go to follow the street shopping.

▼

NT ▶ Next, I'll take the shopping street.

•••

FS ▶ Les boutiques vont ouvrir leurs portes une à une.

LT ▶ The shops go to open their doors one to one.

NT ▶ One by one, the stores will open their doors.

•••

FS ▶ Les vendeurs vont installer leurs étalages colorés de fruits et légumes sur le trottoir.

LT ▶ The sellers go to install their displays colored of fruits and vegetables on the sidewalk.

NT ▶ Vendors will set up their colorful fruit and vegetable stalls on the sidewalk.

•••

FS ▶ Je vais peut-être acheter quelques fruits frais pour mon casse-croûte de midi.

LT ▶ I go perhaps to buy some fruits fresh for my snack of noon.

NT ▶ Maybe I'll buy some fresh fruit for my lunch snack.

•••

FS ▶ Le fleuriste du coin va arranger ses bouquets devant sa devanture.

LT ▶ The florist of the corner goes to arrange his bouquets in front of his storefront.

NT ▶ The local florist will be arranging his bouquets outside their storefront.

•••

FS ▶ Ses fleurs vont apporter une touche de couleur à la rue grise.

LT ▶ His flowers go to bring a touch of color to the street gray.

▼

NT ▶ His flowers will bring a touch of color to the gray street.

•••

FS ▶ Vers midi, je vais me rendre au parc municipal.

LT ▶ Towards noon, I go myself to go to the park municipal.

▼

NT ▶ Around noon, I'm going to head to the municipal park.

•••

FS ▶ Il va être rempli de familles et de personnes qui font leur jogging, profitant du beau temps.

LT ▶ It goes be filled of families and of persons who make their jogging, profiting of the beautiful weather.

NT ▶ It's going to be full of families and joggers, enjoying the fine weather.

•••

FS ▶ Les enfants vont jouer sur les balançoires et le toboggan.

LT ▶ The children go to play on the swings and the slide.

NT ▶ The kids will be playing on the swings and slide.

•••

FS ▶ Un couple va pique-niquer sur l'herbe verte.

LT ▶ A couple goes to picnic on the grass green.

NT ▶ A couple will be picnicking on the green grass.

•••

FS ▶ Vais-je trouver un banc libre pour manger mon casse-croûte ?

LT ▶ Go I to find a bench free for eat my snack?

NT ▶ Will I find a free bench to eat my snack?

•••

FS ▶ Dans l'après-midi, je vais visiter le musée d'art moderne.

LT ▶ In the afternoon, I go to visit the museum of art modern.

NT ▶ In the afternoon, I'll visit the Museum of Modern Art.

•••

FS ▶ Une nouvelle exposition va ouvrir ses portes.

LT ▶ A new exhibition goes to open its doors.

NT ▶ A new exhibition is about to open.

•••

FS ▶ Les œuvres vont sûrement être intéressantes, mais vais-je tout comprendre ?

LT ▶ The artworks go surely be interesting, but go I all to understand?

NT ▶ The artworks will certainly be interesting, but will I understand everything?

•••

FS ▶ Le guide va certainement pouvoir m'expliquer les pièces les plus difficiles.

LT ▶ The guide goes certainly to be able to me explain the pieces the most difficult.

NT ▶ The guide will certainly be able to explain the most difficult pieces to me.

•••

FS ▶ Pour terminer ma journée, je vais prendre le tramway jusqu'au vieux quartier.

LT ▶ For finish my day, I go to take the tramway until to the old neighborhood.

▼

NT ▶ To round off my day, I'll take the streetcar to the old town.

•••

FS ▶ Les rues pavées vont être animées par les terrasses des cafés.

LT ▶ The streets paved go to be animated by the terraces of the cafes.

▼

NT ▶ The cobbled streets will be alive with café terraces.

•••

FS ▶ Les musiciens de rue vont jouer leurs mélodies entraînantes.

LT ▶ The musicians of street go to play their melodies lively.

NT ▶ Street musicians will play their lively melodies.

•••

FS ▶ Le soleil couchant va dorer les façades des vieilles maisons.

LT ▶ The sun setting goes to gild the facades of the old houses.

NT ▶ The setting sun will gild the facades of the old houses.

•••

FS ▶ Quel restaurant vais-je choisir pour dîner ? Il y en a tellement !

LT ▶ Which restaurant go I to choose for dinner? It there of them has so many!

NT ▶ Which restaurant will I choose for dinner? There are so many!

•••

FS ▶ En rentrant, je vais passer par le pont qui passe au-dessus de la rivière.

LT ▶ In returning, I go to pass by the bridge which passes at above of the river.

NT ▶ On my way home, I'll cross the bridge over the river.

•••

FS ▶ Les lumières de la ville vont se refléter dans l'eau, créant un spectacle magique.

LT ▶ The lights of the city go themselves to reflect in the water, creating a spectacle magic.

▼

NT ▶ The city's lights will reflect off the water, creating a magical sight.

•••

FS ▶ Un bateau-mouche va glisser silencieusement sous le pont, transportant des touristes émerveillés.

LT ▶ A boat fly goes to slide silently under the bridge, transporting of the tourists marveled.

▼

NT ▶ A riverboat will glide silently under the bridge, carrying amazed tourists.

•••

FS ▶ Cette journée promet d'être riche en découvertes et en rencontres.

LT ▶ This day promises of be rich in discoveries and in encounters.

NT ▶ The day promises to be rich in discoveries and encounters.

•••

FS ▶ La ville va dévoiler ses secrets au fil de mes pas.

LT ▶ The city goes to unveil its secrets at the thread of my steps.

▼

NT ▶ The city will reveal its secrets as I walk along.

•••

FS ▶ Quels souvenirs vais-je garder de cette promenade ?

LT ▶ Which memories go I to keep of this walk?

▼

NT ▶ What memories will I take away from this walk?

•••

FS ▶ Une chose est sûre, je vais voir ma ville d'un œil nouveau.

LT ▶ One thing is sure, I go to see my city of an eye new.

▼

NT ▶ One thing's for sure, I'll see my city in an entirely new way.

•••

Put Your Learning to the Test

1. Translate the following sentences using the vocabulary from the story:

a) L'odeur du pain frais va remplir la rue quand le boulanger ouvrira sa boutique.

____

b) Je vais acheter des fruits frais sur le marché pour mon casse-croûte de midi..

____

c) Les musiciens de rue vont jouer de belles mélodies sur les places animées.

____

d) Le soir, les lumières de la ville vont se refléter dans la rivière.

____

2. Rearrange the order of the following words to form a correct sentence:

a) vais matin tôt promenade le ma commencer Je

____

b) installer Les leurs fruits le vendeurs trottoir sur vont

____

c) parc midi, me vais À municipal rendre je au

____

d) vais Je illuminées lumières la voir les ville de

____

3. Translate the following words from English to French:

a) baker __________ d) display stand __________

b) fountain __________ e) river __________

c) museum __________ f) terrace __________

4. What does the narrator plan to do in the afternoon?

a) Visit an art museum.

b) Go shopping.

c) Take a boat ride on the river.

d) Have a picnic with a friend.

5. Determine if the following statements are true or false:

a) ______ The narrator plans to start the day with a late breakfast.

b) ______ In the old town, street musicians might be playing lively music.

c) ______ Buying flowers at the florist is part of the planned activities.

d) ______ Before returning home, a bridge over the river will be crossed.

Review your answers on the next page.

Answer Key

1. a) The smell of fresh bread will fill the street when the baker opens his shop.

   b) I will buy fresh fruit at the market for my midday snack.

   c) Street musicians will play beautiful melodies in lively squares.

   d) In the evening, the city lights will reflect in the river.

2. a) Je vais commencer ma promenade tôt le matin.

   b) Les vendeurs vont installer leurs fruits sur le trottoir.

   c) À midi, je vais me rendre au parc municipal.

   d) Je vais voir les lumières illuminées de la ville.

3. a) boulanger b) fontaine c) musée

   d) étalage e) rivière f) terrasse

4. a) Visit an art museum.

5. a) False b) True c) False d) True

10

Main verb tense:
Present simple and Near future
(Présent de l'indicatif et Futur proche)

Persons:
1st person singular
(1ère personne du singulier)

Text type:
Weekly schedule
(Emploi du temps hebdomadaire)

Vocabulary theme:
Days of the week, various activities, hours
(Jours de la semaine, activités variées, heures)

Listening to the story is key to mastering pronunciation and an essential step in your learning journey.

- Start with **slow audio** if you need extra clarity.
- Listen at **normal speed** to get used to natural French.
- Challenge yourself with **fast audio** when you're ready.
- **Practice pronunciation:** Pause after each sentence and repeat it out loud!

Find the audio download on page 12.

Mon emploi du temps de la semaine

Chaque semaine, ma vie suit un rythme bien établi, mais avec toujours quelques surprises. Voici à quoi ressemble mon emploi du temps.

Le lundi, je commence toujours la semaine au bureau à 9h. C'est souvent une journée chargée, remplie de réunions et de planification pour la semaine.

Après le travail, je me détends avec mon cours de yoga à 18h30. Je me demande souvent si je vais enfin réussir la posture du scorpion cette semaine.

Le mardi, je travaille généralement de la maison. C'est une journée plus calme où je peux me concentrer sur mes projets. À midi, je déjeune souvent avec ma voisine, ce qui me permet de faire une pause agréable.

Ce mardi, je vais aller au cinéma voir le nouveau film français dont tout le monde parle. Avec qui vais-je y aller ? Je n'ai pas encore décidé.

Le mercredi est toujours une journée chargée. Je commence tôt, à 8h, pour une réunion importante. Après une longue journée de travail, je fais habituellement les courses pour la semaine.

Cette fois-ci, je vais essayer de nouveaux ingrédients. Qu'est-ce que je vais acheter pour varier mes menus ?

Le jeudi, je travaille jusqu'à 16h. Cette semaine, j'ai un rendez-vous chez le dentiste à 17h, ce qui n'est pas mon moment préféré.

Pour me remonter le moral, je vais préparer un dîner pour mes amis le soir. Je réfléchis déjà à ce que je vais cuisiner pour les impressionner.

Vendredi, c'est le dernier jour de travail de la semaine ! Je finis à 17h et je file à ma leçon de piano à 18h. J'adore terminer la semaine en musique.

Ce vendredi, je vais sortir avec des collègues pour fêter un projet réussi. Où allons-nous aller ? C'est encore un mystère.

Le samedi est mon jour de repos. Je fais la grasse matinée et je prends tranquillement mon petit-déjeuner. L'après-midi, je vais souvent à la bibliothèque.

Cette fois, je vais rendre mes livres et en emprunter de nouveaux. Je me demande quels genres de livres vont attirer mon attention.

Le dimanche, je commence la journée par une visite au marché pour acheter des produits frais. Mes parents viennent déjeuner ce dimanche, alors je vais préparer un repas spécial.

L'après-midi, je fais toujours une longue promenade dans le parc, c'est ma façon de me ressourcer et mon moment préféré de la semaine.

Le soir, je prépare mes affaires pour la semaine à venir, en réfléchissant à la meilleure façon de m'organiser pour être productive.

Cette semaine, je vais aussi essayer de trouver un moment pour appeler ma sœur qui habite à l'étranger. Avec le décalage horaire, ce n'est pas toujours facile. Quand vais-je pouvoir la joindre ? Je dois encore jongler avec nos emplois du temps respectifs.

Ainsi se déroule ma semaine, un mélange de routine et de petites aventures quotidiennes.

Explore the Translation

FS ▶ Mon emploi du temps de la semaine

LT ▶ My schedule of time of the week

NT ▶ My weekly schedule

•••

FS ▶ Chaque semaine, ma vie suit un rythme bien établi, mais avec toujours quelques surprises.

LT ▶ Each week, my life follows a rhythm well established, but with always some surprises.

▼

NT ▶ Every week, my life follows a well-established rhythm, but there are always a few surprises.

•••

FS ▶ Voici à quoi ressemble mon emploi du temps.

LT ▶ Here is to what looks like my schedule.

NT ▶ Here's what my schedule looks like.

•••

FS ▶ Le lundi, je commence toujours la semaine au bureau à 9h.

LT ▶ The Monday, I begin always the week at the office at 9 a.m

NT ▶ On Mondays, I always start the week at the office at 9 a.m.

•••

FS ▶ C'est souvent une journée chargée, remplie de réunions et de planification pour la semaine.

LT ▶ It is often a day busy, filled of meetings and of planning for the week.

NT ▶ It's usually a busy day, full of meetings and planning for the week ahead.

•••

FS ▶ Après le travail, je me détends avec mon cours de yoga à 18h30.

LT ▶ After the work, I myself relax with my course of yoga at 6:30 p.m.

NT ▶ After work, I relax with my yoga class at 6:30 p.m.

•••

FS ▶ Je me demande souvent si je vais enfin réussir la posture du scorpion cette semaine.

LT ▶ I myself ask often if I go finally to succeed the posture of the scorpion this week.

NT ▶ I often wonder if I'll finally get the scorpion pose right this week.

•••

FS ▶ Le mardi, je travaille généralement de la maison.

LT ▶ The Tuesday, I work generally from the house.

NT ▶ On Tuesdays, I usually work from home.

•••

FS ▶ C'est une journée plus calme où je peux me concentrer sur mes projets.

LT ▶ It is a day more calm where I can myself concentrate on my projects.

NT ▶ It's a quieter day when I can focus on my projects.

•••

FS ▶ À midi, je déjeune souvent avec ma voisine, ce qui me permet de faire une pause agréable.

LT ▶ At noon, I lunch often with my neighbor, which me allows to make a break pleasant.

NT ▶ At lunchtime, I often have lunch with my neighbor, which gives me a nice break.

•••

FS ▶ Ce mardi, je vais aller au cinéma voir le nouveau film français dont tout le monde parle.

LT ▶ This Tuesday, I 'm going to go to the cinema to see the new film French which everyone speaks.

NT ▶ This Tuesday, I'm going to the cinema to see the new French film everyone's talking about.

•••

FS ▶ Avec qui vais-je y aller ? Je n'ai pas encore décidé.

LT ▶ With whom will I there go? I have not yet decided.

NT ▶ Who am I going with? I haven't decided yet.

•••

FS ▶ Le mercredi est toujours une journée chargée. Je commence tôt, à 8h, pour une réunion importante.

LT ▶ The Wednesday is always a day busy. I begin early, at 8 a.m., for a meeting important.

NT ▶ Wednesday is always a busy day. I start early, at 8 a.m., for an important meeting.

•••

FS ▶ Après une longue journée de travail, je fais habituellement les courses pour la semaine.

LT ▶ After a long day of work, I do usually the shopping for the week.

NT ▶ After a long day at work, I usually do the shopping for the week.

•••

FS ▶ Cette fois-ci, je vais essayer de nouveaux ingrédients.

LT ▶ This time, I go to try of new ingredients.

NT ▶ This time, I'm going to try some new ingredients.

•••

FS ▶ Qu'est-ce que je vais acheter pour varier mes menus ?

LT ▶ What is it that I go to buy for vary my menus?

NT ▶ What will I buy to vary my menus?

•••

FS ▶ Le jeudi, je travaille jusqu'à 16h.

LT ▶ The Thursday, I work until 4 p.m.

NT ▶ On Thursdays, I work until 4 p.m.

FS ▶ Cette semaine, j'ai un rendez-vous chez le dentiste à 17h, ce qui n'est pas mon moment préféré.

LT ▶ This week, I have an appointment at the dentist at 5 p.m., that which is not my moment preferred.

▼

NT ▶ This week, I have a dentist's appointment at 5 p.m., which is not my favorite time.

FS ▶ Pour me remonter le moral, je vais préparer un dîner pour mes amis le soir.

LT ▶ For myself to raise the morale, I go to prepare a dinner for my friends the evening.

▼

NT ▶ To cheer myself up, I'm going to cook dinner for my friends in the evening.

FS ▶ Je réfléchis déjà à ce que je vais cuisiner pour les impressionner.

LT ▶ I think already to what I go to cook for them to impress.

▼

NT ▶ I'm already thinking about what I'm going to cook to impress them.

FS ▶ Vendredi, c'est le dernier jour de travail de la semaine !

LT ▶ Friday, it is the last day of work of the week!

▼

NT ▶ Friday is the last working day of the week!

•••

FS ▶ Je finis à 17h et je file à ma leçon de piano à 18h. J'adore terminer la semaine en musique.

LT ▶ I finish at 5 p.m. and I rush to my lesson of piano at 6 p.m. I love to finish the week in music.

▼

NT ▶ I finish at 5 p.m. and head off to my piano lesson at 6 p.m. I love ending the week with music.

•••

FS ▶ Ce vendredi, je vais sortir avec des collègues pour fêter un projet réussi.

LT ▶ This Friday, I go to go out with some colleagues for celebrate a project succeeded.

NT ▶ This Friday, I'm going out with some colleagues to celebrate a successful project.

•••

FS ▶ Où allons-nous aller ? C'est encore un mystère.

LT ▶ Where go we to go? It is still a mystery.

NT ▶ Where will we go? That's still a mystery.

•••

FS ▶ Le samedi est mon jour de repos. Je fais la grasse matinée et je prends tranquillement mon petit-déjeuner.

LT ▶ The Saturday is my day of rest. I do the lazy morning and I take calmly my breakfast.

NT ▶ Saturday is my day off. I sleep in and have a quiet breakfast.

•••

FS ▶ L'après-midi, je vais souvent à la bibliothèque.

LT ▶ The afternoon, I go often to the library.

▼

NT ▶ In the afternoon, I often go to the library.

•••

FS ▶ Cette fois, je vais rendre mes livres et en emprunter de nouveaux.

LT ▶ This time, I go to return my books and of them borrow of new.

NT ▶ This time, I'm returning my books and borrowing new ones.

•••

FS ▶ Je me demande quels genres de livres vont attirer mon attention.

LT ▶ I myself ask what kinds of books go to attract my attention.

NT ▶ I wonder what kind of books will catch my attention.

•••

FS ▶ Le dimanche, je commence la journée par une visite au marché pour acheter des produits frais.

LT ▶ The Sunday, I begin the day by a visit to the market to buy some products fresh.

NT ▶ On Sundays, I start the day with a trip to the market to buy fresh produce.

•••

FS ▶ Mes parents viennent déjeuner ce dimanche, alors je vais préparer un repas spécial.

LT ▶ My parents come to lunch this Sunday, then I go to prepare a meal special.

NT ▶ My parents are coming for lunch this Sunday, so I'll prepare a special meal.

•••

FS ▶ L'après-midi, je fais toujours une longue promenade dans le parc, c'est ma façon de me ressourcer et mon moment préféré de la semaine.

LT ▶ The afternoon, I do always a long walk in the park, it is my way of myself to recharge and my moment preferred of the week.

▼

NT ▶ In the afternoon, I always take a long walk in the park; it's my way of recharging my batteries and my favorite part of the week.

•••

FS ▶ Le soir, je prépare mes affaires pour la semaine à venir, en réfléchissant à la meilleure façon de m'organiser pour être productive.

LT ▶ The evening, I prepare my things for the week to come, in thinking to the best way of myself to organize for be productive.

▼

NT ▶ In the evening, I prepare my things for the week ahead, thinking about how best to organize myself to be productive.

•••

FS ▶ Cette semaine, je vais aussi essayer de trouver un moment pour appeler ma sœur qui habite à l'étranger.

LT ▶ This week, I go also to try to find a moment for call my sister who lives abroad.

▼

NT ▶ This week, I'm also going to try to find a time to call my sister who lives abroad.

•••

FS ▶ Avec le décalage horaire, ce n'est pas toujours facile. Quand vais-je pouvoir la joindre ?

LT ▶ With the gap hourly, It is not always easy. When go I to be able her to join?

▼

NT ▶ With the time difference, it's not always easy. When will I be able to reach her?

•••

FS ▶ Je dois encore jongler avec nos emplois du temps respectifs.

LT ▶ I must still juggle with our schedules respective.

NT ▶ I still have to juggle our respective schedules.

•••

FS ▶ Ainsi se déroule ma semaine, un mélange de routine et de petites aventures quotidiennes.

LT ▶ Thus itself unfolds my week, a mixture of routine and of small adventures daily.

NT ▶ And so my week unfolds, a mixture of routine and small daily adventures.

•••

Put Your Learning to the Test

1. Translate the following sentences using the vocabulary from the story:

a) Le lundi, je commence ma semaine au bureau avec des réunions importantes.

____

b) Après le travail, je vais à mon cours de yoga pour me détendre.

____

c) Le samedi après-midi, je vais rendre mes livres et en emprunter de nouveaux.

____

d) Dimanche, je vais au marché pour acheter des produits frais avant de préparer un repas.

____

2. Rearrange the order of the following words to form a correct sentence:

a) commence bureau je toujours semaine la au lundi Le

____

b) travail Après yoga le vais je cours mon à de

____

c) vais je bibliothèque souvent la à après-midi L'

____

d) affaires prépare Je semaine pour mes la venir à

____

3. Translate the following words from French to English:

a) réunion	__________	d) bibliothèque	__________
b) projet	__________	e) marché	__________
c) dentiste	__________	f) promenade	__________

4. Determine if the following statements are true or false:

a) ______ The narrator starts work at 10 a.m. on Monday.

b) ______ On Tuesday, a movie night is planned.

c) ______ Parents are invited for lunch on Sunday.

d) ______ Music is part of the Friday routine.

Review your answers on the next page.

Answer Key

1. a) On Monday, I start my week at the office with important meetings.

   b) After work, I go to my yoga class to relax.

   c) On Saturday afternoon, I will return my books and borrow new ones.

   d) On Sunday, I go to the market to buy fresh products before preparing a meal.

2. a) Le lundi, je commence toujours la semaine au bureau.

   b) Après le travail, je vais à mon cours de yoga.

   c) L'après-midi, je vais souvent à la bibliothèque.

   d) Je prépare mes affaires pour la semaine à venir.

3. a) meeting b) project c) dentist

   d) library e) market f) walk or stroll

4. a) False b) True c) True d) True

SHORT STORY

11

Main verb tenses:
Near future, Present tense, Imperative
(Futur proche, Présent de l'indicatif, Impératif)

Main person:
1st person plural
(1ère personne du pluriel)

Text type:
Planning guide
(Guide de planification)

Vocabulary theme:
Parties and celebrations
(Fêtes et célébrations)

Listening to the story is key to mastering pronunciation and an essential step in your learning journey.

- Start with **slow audio** if you need extra clarity.
- Listen at **normal speed** to get used to natural French.
- Challenge yourself with **fast audio** when you're ready.
- **Practice pronunciation:** Pause after each sentence and repeat it out loud!

Find the audio download on page 12.

Planifions notre fête !

Pour organiser notre fête, nous allons suivre ce guide étape par étape. N'oublions pas que la clé d'une fête réussie est une bonne organisation !

1. Invitations : Nous allons commencer par établir la liste des invités. N'invitons pas trop de monde, notre espace est limité. Ensuite, nous allons créer des invitations. Soyons créatifs ! N'oublions pas d'inclure la date, l'heure et l'adresse.

2. Décoration : Nous allons choisir un thème pour notre fête. Ne négligeons pas l'ambiance, c'est important ! Nous allons acheter ou fabriquer des décorations en accord avec notre thème. Accrochons des guirlandes, gonflons des ballons et créons une belle table d'accueil.

3. Musique : Nous allons préparer une playlist variée. N'hésitons pas à demander à nos invités leurs chansons préférées. Vérifions que notre système audio fonctionne bien avant la fête.

4. Nourriture et boissons : Nous allons préparer un buffet. Pensons à varier les plats : crudités, brochettes et mini-pizzas. N'oublions pas les options végétariennes ! Pour les boissons, nous allons prévoir des options avec et sans alcool. Achetons plus que nécessaire, il vaut mieux avoir trop que pas assez.

5. Activités : Nous allons planifier quelques jeux ou activités. Ne laissons pas nos invités s'ennuyer ! Nous allons préparer un jeu de questions-réponses amusant ou un jeu de société. Adaptons les activités à nos invités.

6. Préparation de l'espace : Nous allons réorganiser les meubles pour créer de l'espace. Nous allons désigner des zones : une pour danser, une pour le buffet, et des coins plus calmes pour discuter. N'oublions pas de prévoir suffisamment de places assises.

7. Derniers préparatifs : Le jour J, nous allons tout mettre en place. Nous allons décorer la salle, préparer le buffet et vérifier une dernière fois que tout est prêt. N'attendons pas la dernière minute pour ces préparatifs !

8. Accueil des invités : Nous allons être prêts à accueillir nos invités chaleureusement. Nous allons leur proposer un verre dès leur arrivée et les présenter aux autres personnes. Créons une atmosphère conviviale dès le début.

9. Pendant la fête : Nous allons veiller à ce que tout se passe bien. Nous allons nous assurer que le buffet reste garni et que la musique continue. N'hésitons pas à lancer des activités si l'ambiance baisse.

10. Après la fête : Nous allons prévoir le nettoyage. Ne laissons pas tout pour le lendemain ! Nous allons demander à quelques amis de rester pour nous aider.

En suivant ce guide, notre fête sera sûrement un succès. Amusons-nous bien et créons de beaux souvenirs !

Explore the Translation

FS ▶ Planifions notre fête !

LT ▶ Let us plan our party!

NT ▶ Let's plan our party!

•••

FS ▶ Pour organiser notre fête, nous allons suivre ce guide étape par étape.

LT ▶ For organize our party, we go to follow this guide step by step.

NT ▶ To organize our party, we're going to follow this step-by-step guide.

•••

FS ▶ N'oublions pas que la clé d'une fête réussie est une bonne organisation !

LT ▶ Let us forget not that the key of a party successful is a good organization!

▼

NT ▶ Remember that the key to a successful party is good organization!

◆◆◆

FS ▶ 1. Invitations : Nous allons commencer par établir la liste des invités.

LT ▶ 1. Invitations: We go to begin by to establish the list of the guests.

▼

NT ▶ 1. Invitations: We'll begin by putting together the guest list.

◆◆◆

FS ▶ N'invitons pas trop de monde, notre espace est limité.

LT ▶ We invite not too much people, our space is limited.

▼

NT ▶ Let's not invite too many people since our space is limited.

◆◆◆

FS ▶ Ensuite, nous allons créer des invitations. Soyons créatifs !

LT ▶ Then, we go to create some invitations. Let's be creative!

NT ▶ Next, we're going to create the invitations. Let's get creative!

◆◆◆

FS ▶ N'oublions pas d'inclure la date, l'heure et l'adresse.

LT ▶ Let us forget not include the date, the hour, and the address.

NT ▶ Don't forget to include the date, time, and address.

◆◆◆

FS ▶ 2. Décoration : Nous allons choisir un thème pour notre fête.

LT ▶ 2. Decoration: We go to choose a theme for our party.

▼

NT ▶ 2. Decoration: We'll choose a theme for the party.

◆◆◆

FS ▶ Ne négligeons pas l'ambiance, c'est important !

LT ▶ Let us neglect not the atmosphere, it is important!

NT ▶ Let's not overlook the atmosphere, it's important!

•••

FS ▶ Nous allons acheter ou fabriquer des décorations en accord avec notre thème.

LT ▶ We go to buy or make some decorations in accordance with our theme.

NT ▶ We're going to buy or make decorations that match the theme.

•••

FS ▶ Accrochons des guirlandes, gonflons des ballons et créons une belle table d'accueil.

LT ▶ Let us hang some garlands, inflate some balloons, and create a beautiful table of reception.

NT ▶ Let's hang garlands, blow up balloons, and set up a beautiful welcome table.

•••

FS ▶ 3. Musique : Nous allons préparer une playlist variée.

LT ▶ 3. Music: We go to prepare a playlist varied.

NT ▶ 3. Music: We're going to prepare a diverse playlist.

•••

FS ▶ N'hésitons pas à demander à nos invités leurs chansons préférées.

LT ▶ Let us hesitate not to ask to our guests their songs preferred.

NT ▶ Let's not hesitate to ask our guests for their favorite songs.

•••

FS ▶ Vérifions que notre système audio fonctionne bien avant la fête.

LT ▶ Let us check that our system audio works well before the party.

▼

NT ▶ Let's make sure our sound system is working properly before the party.

•••

FS ▶ 4. Nourriture et boissons :Nous allons préparer un buffet.

LT ▶ 4. Food and drinks: We go to prepare a buffet.

▼

NT ▶ 4. Food and beverages: We're going to prepare a buffet.

•••

FS ▶ Pensons à varier les plats : crudités, brochettes et mini-pizzas.

LT ▶ Let us think to vary the dishes: raw vegetables, skewers, and mini pizzas.

NT ▶ Let's vary the dishes: raw veggies, skewers, and mini pizzas.

•••

FS ▶ N'oublions pas les options végétariennes !

LT ▶ Let us forget not the options vegetarian!

NT ▶ We won't forget the vegetarian options!

•••

FS ▶ Pour les boissons, nous allons prévoir des options avec et sans alcool.

LT ▶ For the drinks, we go to plan options with and without alcohol.

▼

NT ▶ For drinks, we're going to have both alcoholic and non-alcoholic options.

•••

FS ▶ Achetons plus que nécessaire, il vaut mieux avoir trop que pas assez.

LT ▶ Let us buy more than necessary, it is better to have too much than not enough.

▼

NT ▶ Let's buy more than we need, it's better to have too much than not enough.

•••

FS ▶ 5. Activités : Nous allons planifier quelques jeux ou activités.

LT ▶ 5. Activities: We go to plan some games or activities.

▼

NT ▶ 5. Activities: We're going to plan some games or activities.

•••

FS ▶ Ne laissons pas nos invités s'ennuyer !

LT ▶ Let us leave not our guests themselves to bore!

▼

NT ▶ Let's make sure our guests don't get bored!

•••

FS ▶ Nous allons préparer un jeu de questions-réponses amusant ou un jeu de société.

LT ▶ We go to prepare a game of questions-answers fun or a game of society.

NT ▶ We're going to prepare a fun trivia game or a board game.

•••

FS ▶ Adaptons les activités à nos invités.

LT ▶ Let us adapt the activities to our guests.

▼

NT ▶ Let's tailor the activities to our guests.

•••

FS ▶ 6. Préparation de l'espace : Nous allons réorganiser les meubles pour créer de l'espace.

LT ▶ 6. Preparation of the space: We go to reorganize the furniture to create of the space.

▼

NT ▶ 6. Space preparation: We're going to rearrange the furniture to make more room.

•••

FS ▶ Nous allons désigner des zones : une pour danser, une pour le buffet, et des coins plus calmes pour discuter.

LT ▶ We go to designate zones: one for dancing, one for the buffet, and corners calmer for to discuss.

▼

NT ▶ We're going to set up areas for dancing, the buffet, and quiet corners to chat.

•••

FS ▶ N'oublions pas de prévoir suffisamment de places assises.

LT ▶ Let us forget not to plan enough places seated.

NT ▶ Don't forget to provide enough seating.

•••

FS ▶ 7. Derniers préparatifs : Le jour J, nous allons tout mettre en place. Nous allons décorer la salle.

LT ▶ 7. Last preparations : The Day D, we go to put everything in place. We go to decorate the room.

▼

NT ▶ 7. Final preparations: On the big day, we're going to set everything up. We're going to decorate the space.

•••

FS ▶ Nous allons préparer le buffet et vérifier une dernière fois que tout est prêt.

LT ▶ We go to prepare the buffet and to verify one last time that everything is ready.

NT ▶ We're going to prepare the buffet, and double-check that everything is ready.

•••

FS ▶ N'attendons pas la dernière minute pour ces préparatifs !

LT ▶ Let us wait not for the last minute for these preparations!

NT ▶ We won't wait until the last minute to complete these tasks!

•••

FS ▶ 8. Accueil des invités : Nous allons être prêts à accueillir nos invités chaleureusement.

LT ▶ 8. Welcome of the guests: We go to be ready to welcome our guests warmly.

NT ▶ 8. Welcoming guests: We're going to be ready to greet our guests warmly.

•••

FS ▶ Nous allons leur proposer un verre dès leur arrivée et les présenter aux autres personnes.

LT ▶ We go to propose them a drink from their arrival and present them to the other people.

NT ▶ We're going to greet guests with a drink and introduce them to each other.

•••

FS ▶ Créons une atmosphère conviviale dès le début.

LT ▶ Let us create a friendly atmosphere from the beginning.

▼

NT ▶ Let's create a friendly atmosphere right from the start.

•••

FS ▶ 9. Pendant la fête : Nous allons veiller à ce que tout se passe bien.

LT ▶ 9. During the party: We go to watch that everything happens well.

▼

NT ▶ 9. During the party: We're going to make sure everything runs smoothly.

•••

FS ▶ Nous allons nous assurer que le buffet reste garni et que la musique continue.

LT ▶ We go to ensure that the buffet stays filled and that the music continues.

NT ▶ We're going to keep the buffet stocked and the music going.

•••

FS ▶ N'hésitons pas à lancer des activités si l'ambiance baisse.

LT ▶ Let us hesitate not to launch activities if the atmosphere drops.

▼

NT ▶ Let's not hesitate to start some activities if the mood drops.

•••

FS ▶ 10. Après la fête : Nous allons prévoir le nettoyage. Ne laissons pas tout pour le lendemain !

LT ▶ 10. After the party: We go to foresee the cleaning. Let us leave not everything for the next day!

▼

NT ▶ 10. After the party: We're going to plan for cleanup. We won't leave everything for the next day!

•••

FS ▶ Nous allons demander à quelques amis de rester pour nous aider.

LT ▶ We go to ask some friends to stay for help us.

▼

NT ▶ We're going to ask a few friends to stay and help us out.

•••

FS ▶ En suivant ce guide, notre fête sera sûrement un succès.

LT/NT ▶ By following this guide, our party will be surely a success.

•••

FS ▶ Amusons-nous bien et créons de beaux souvenirs !

LT ▶ Let us amuse ourselves well and create some beautiful memories!

NT ▶ Let's have fun and make wonderful memories!

•••

Put Your Learning to the Test

1. Translate the following sentences using the vocabulary from the story:

a) Nous allons établir une liste d'invités avant d'envoyer les invitations.

____

b) Pour l'ambiance, nous allons accrocher des guirlandes et gonfler des ballons.

____

c) Il faut prévoir des boissons avec et sans alcool pour nos invités.

____

d) Après la fête, nous allons nettoyer et remettre la salle en ordre.

____

2. Rearrange the order of the following words to form a correct sentence:

a) invités liste établir allons une Nous d'

____

b) buffet le préparer allons Nous avant fête la

____

c) soirée Pendant musique la bonne une assurer allons nous

____

d) invités accueillir Nous les chaleureusement allons

____

3. Circle the odd one out:

a) ballons - lumières - minute - guirlandes

b) musique - crudités - brochettes - pizza

c) conviviale - invitation - amusant - variée

d) organiser - cuisiner - chaise - nettoyer

4. Determine if the following statements are true or false:

a) _______ The first step of planning is to buy decorations.

b) _______ A playlist will be prepared before the party.

c) _______ The host will provide only alcoholic drinks.

d) _______ Guests will be welcomed warmly when they arrive.

Review your answers on the next page.

Answer Key

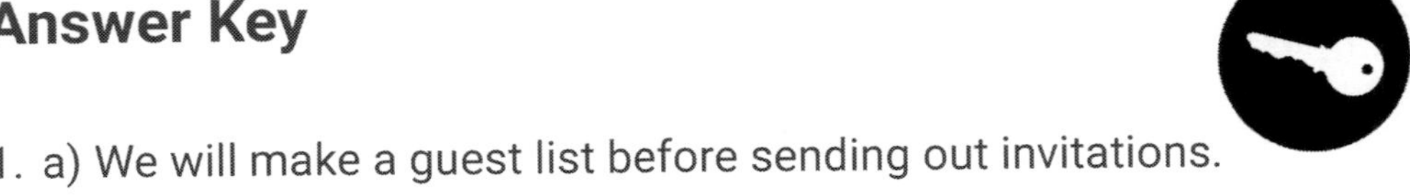

1. a) We will make a guest list before sending out invitations.

   b) For the atmosphere, we will hang garlands and inflate balloons.

   c) We must plan for both alcoholic and non-alcoholic drinks for our guests.

   d) After the party, we will clean up and put everything back in order.

2. a) Nous allons établir une liste d'invités.

   b) Nous allons préparer le buffet avant la fête.

   c) Pendant la soirée, nous allons assurer une bonne musique.

   d) Nous allons accueillir les invités chaleureusement.

3. a) Minute
   The others are decorations, but "minute" is related to time.

   b) Musique
   The others are types of food, but "musique" is entertainment.

   c) Invitation
   The others are adjectives, but "invitation" is a noun.

   d) Chaise
   The others are verbs, but "chaise" is an object.

4. a) False b) True c) False d) True

Main verb tense:
Near future
(Futur proche)

Main person:
3rd person singular
(3ème personne du singulier)

Text type:
Weather forecast
(Prévisions météorologiques)

Vocabulary theme:
Seasons and weather
(Saisons et météo)

Listening to the story is key to mastering pronunciation and an essential step in your learning journey.

- Start with **slow audio** if you need extra clarity.
- Listen at **normal speed** to get used to natural French.
- Challenge yourself with **fast audio** when you're ready.
- **Practice pronunciation:** Pause after each sentence and repeat it out loud!

Find the audio download on page 12.

Prévisions météorologiques en France

Bonjour à tous ! Voici les prévisions météorologiques pour les quatre saisons à venir en France. Ces prévisions donneront un aperçu général du temps à travers le pays, tout en mentionnant quelques particularités régionales.

Pour commencer, parlons du printemps qui va bientôt arriver. Le temps va se réchauffer progressivement. Les températures vont osciller entre 10°C et 20°C.

Il va pleuvoir fréquemment, mais ces averses seront bénéfiques pour la nature qui va se réveiller. Les arbres vont bourgeonner et les premières fleurs vont éclore. On va pouvoir ranger les manteaux d'hiver, mais il sera encore prudent de garder un parapluie à portée de main.

Les arbres fruitiers vont se couvrir de fleurs délicates. Va-t-on voir les premières jonquilles percer dans les jardins, annonçant l'arrivée du printemps ?

L'été va suivre avec des journées qui vont s'allonger. Le soleil va briller intensément et les températures vont grimper, atteignant parfois 30°C. Il va faire chaud et sec.

On va pouvoir sortir les vêtements légers : shorts, t-shirts et robes d'été. Les champs de blé vont jaunir sous le soleil. Les insectes, comme les abeilles et les papillons, vont être très actifs.

Dans les régions du sud, on va entendre le chant caractéristique des cigales. Sera-t-il nécessaire d'arroser plus souvent les jardins pour compenser le manque de pluie ?

L'automne va ensuite s'installer progressivement. Les températures vont baisser, oscillant entre 5°C et 15°C. Le temps va devenir plus variable, avec un mélange de journées ensoleillées et pluvieuses.

Les feuilles des arbres vont changer de couleur, passant du vert au jaune, à l'orange et au rouge, avant de tomber. Il va falloir ressortir les pulls et les vestes légères.

Les oiseaux migrateurs vont se préparer pour leur long voyage vers le sud. Va-t-on voir les volées d'oies sauvages dans le ciel ?

Enfin, l'hiver va arriver avec ses journées courtes et froides. Les températures vont chuter, souvent en dessous de 0°C. Il va neiger dans certaines régions, créant un paysage blanc et silencieux.

On va devoir s'habiller chaudement : manteaux, écharpes, gants et bonnets seront de rigueur. La nature va sembler endormie, mais certains animaux resteront actifs.

Les écureuils vont chercher les provisions qu'ils ont cachées à l'automne. Les oiseaux qui n'ont pas migré vont venir aux mangeoires installées dans les jardins. Comment la faune locale va-t-elle s'adapter à ces conditions difficiles ?

Ces changements de saisons vont influencer non seulement notre façon de nous habiller, mais aussi le comportement des animaux et le cycle de la nature.

Chaque saison va apporter son lot de beautés et de défis. Il sera intéressant d'observer comment la flore et la faune vont s'adapter à ces variations climatiques.

N'oubliez pas de consulter régulièrement les prévisions météo pour vous préparer au mieux aux conditions à venir. Profitez bien de chaque saison !

Explore the Translation

FS ▶ Prévisions météorologiques en France

LT ▶ Forecasts meteorological in France

▼

NT ▶ Weather forecast in France

•••

FS ▶ Bonjour à tous !

LT ▶ Hello to all!

▼

NT ▶ Hello everyone!

FS ▶ Voici les prévisions météorologiques pour les quatre saisons à venir en France.

LT ▶ Here are the forecasts meteorological for the four seasons to come in France.

NT ▶ Here are the weather forecasts for the next four seasons in France.

•••

FS ▶ Ces prévisions donneront un aperçu général du temps à travers le pays, tout en mentionnant quelques particularités régionales.

LT ▶ These forecasts will give an overview general of the weather across the country, all while mentioning some particularities regional.

NT ▶ These forecasts will give a general overview of the weather across the country, while mentioning a few regional differences.

•••

FS ▶ Pour commencer, parlons du printemps qui va bientôt arriver.

LT ▶ To begin, let's talk about the spring that go soon arrive.

NT ▶ To begin with, let's talk about spring, which is just around the corner.

•••

FS ▶ Le temps va se réchauffer progressivement.

LT ▶ The weather go itself to warm gradually.

▼

NT ▶ The weather will gradually warm up.

•••

FS ▶ Les températures vont osciller entre 10°C et 20°C.

LT ▶ The temperatures go to oscillate between 10°C and 20°C.

NT ▶ Temperatures will range between 10°C and 20°C.

•••

FS ▶ Il va pleuvoir fréquemment, mais ces averses seront bénéfiques pour la nature qui va se réveiller.

LT ▶ It goes to rain frequently, but these showers will be beneficial for the nature that goes itself to wake.

▼

NT ▶ It will rain frequently, but these showers will be good for nature, which will be waking up.

•••

FS ▶ Les arbres vont bourgeonner et les premières fleurs vont éclore.

LT ▶ The trees go to bud and the first flowers go to bloom.

NT ▶ The trees will begin to bud and the first flowers will bloom.

•••

FS ▶ On va pouvoir ranger les manteaux d'hiver, mais il sera encore prudent de garder un parapluie à portée de main.

LT ▶ We go to be able to put away the coats of winter, but it will be still wise of to keep an umbrella at reach of hand

NT ▶ We'll be able to put away our winter coats, but it will still be wise to keep an umbrella close at hand.

•••

FS ▶ Les arbres fruitiers vont se couvrir de fleurs délicates.

LT ▶ The trees fruit go to themselves cover of flowers delicate.

▼

NT ▶ The fruit trees will be covered in delicate blossoms.

•••

FS ▶ Va-t-on voir les premières jonquilles percer dans les jardins, annonçant l'arrivée du printemps ?

LT ▶ Go we see the first daffodils to pierce in the gardens, announcing the arrival of spring?

NT ▶ Will we see the first daffodils popping up in the gardens, marking the arrival of spring?

•••

FS ▶ L'été va suivre avec des journées qui vont s'allonger.

LT ▶ The summer goes to follow with some days that will themselves lengthen.

NT ▶ Summer will follow, with longer days ahead.

•••

FS ▶ Le soleil va briller intensément et les températures vont grimper, atteignant parfois 30°C.

LT ▶ The sun goes to shine intensely and the temperatures go to climb, reaching sometimes 30°C.

NT ▶ The sun will shine brightly and temperatures will soar, sometimes reaching 30°C.

•••

FS ▶ Il va faire chaud et sec. On va pouvoir sortir les vêtements légers : shorts, t-shirts et robes d'été.

LT ▶ It goes to make hot and dry. We go to be able to go out the clothes light: shorts, t-shirts and dresses of summer.

▼

NT ▶ The weather will be hot and dry. We'll be able to break out our light clothes: shorts, T-shirts, and summer dresses.

•••

FS ▶ Les champs de blé vont jaunir sous le soleil.

LT ▶ The fields of wheat go to turn yellow under the sun.

NT ▶ Wheat fields will turn golden under the sun.

•••

FS ▶ Les insectes, comme les abeilles et les papillons, vont être très actifs.

LT ▶ The insects, as the bees and the butterflies, go to be very active.

NT ▶ Insects like bees and butterflies will be very active.

•••

FS ▶ Dans les régions du sud, on va entendre le chant caractéristique des cigales.

LT ▶ In the regions of the south, we go to hear the song characteristic of the cicadas.

NT ▶ In the south, the distinctive song of cicadas will be heard.

•••

FS ▶ Sera-t-il nécessaire d'arroser plus souvent les jardins pour compenser le manque de pluie ?

LT ▶ Will it be necessary to water more often the gardens for to compensate the lack of rain?

NT ▶ Will gardens need to be watered more often to make up for the lack of rain?

•••

FS ▶ L'automne va ensuite s'installer progressivement.

LT ▶ The autumn goes then itself to install gradually.

NT ▶ Autumn will then gradually set in.

•••

FS ▶ Les températures vont baisser, oscillant entre 5°C et 15°C.
LT ▶ The temperatures go to lower, oscillating between 5°C and 15°C.
▼
NT ▶ Temperatures will drop, ranging between 5°C and 15°C.

•••

FS ▶ Le temps va devenir plus variable, avec un mélange de journées ensoleillées et pluvieuses.
LT ▶ The weather goes to become more variable, with a mix of days sunny and rainy.
▼
NT ▶ The weather will become more unpredictable, with a mix of sunny and rainy days.

•••

FS ▶ Les feuilles des arbres vont changer de couleur, passant du vert au jaune, à l'orange et au rouge, avant de tomber.
LT ▶ The leaves of the trees go to change of color, passing from the green to the yellow, to the orange and to the red, before of falling.
▼
NT ▶ Tree leaves will change color, turning from green to yellow, orange, and red, before falling.

•••

FS ▶ Il va falloir ressortir les pulls et les vestes légères.
LT ▶ It goes to have to go out again the sweaters and the jackets light.
▼
NT ▶ We're going to need to bring out the sweaters and light jackets again.

•••

FS ▶ Les oiseaux migrateurs vont se préparer pour leur long voyage vers le sud.
LT ▶ The birds migratory go themselves to prepare for their long journey

toward the south.

NT ▶ Migratory birds will be preparing for their long journey south.

•••

FS ▶ Va-t-on voir les volées d'oies sauvages dans le ciel ?

LT ▶ Will we see the flights of geese wild in the sky?

NT ▶ Will we see flocks of wild geese in the sky?

•••

FS ▶ Enfin, l'hiver va arriver avec ses journées courtes et froides.

LT ▶ Finally, the winter goes to arrive with its days short and cold.

NT ▶ Finally, winter will arrive with its short, cold days.

•••

FS ▶ Les températures vont chuter, souvent en dessous de 0°C.

LT ▶ The temperatures go to fall, often below 0°C.

NT ▶ Temperatures will drop, often falling below 0°C.

•••

FS ▶ Il va neiger dans certaines régions, créant un paysage blanc et silencieux.

LT ▶ It goes to snow in certain regions, creating a landscape white and silent.

NT ▶ It will snow in some regions, creating a quiet, snowy landscape.

•••

FS ▶ On va devoir s'habiller chaudement : manteaux, écharpes, gants et bonnets seront de rigueur.

LT ▶ WWe go to must dress warmly: coats, scarves, gloves and hats will be of rigor.

▼

NT ▶ We'll need to dress warmly: coats, scarves, gloves, and hats will be a must.

•••

FS ▶ La nature va sembler endormie, mais certains animaux resteront actifs.

LT ▶ The nature goes to seem asleep, but certain animals will remain active..

NT ▶ Nature will seem dormant, but some animals will remain active.

•••

FS ▶ Les écureuils vont chercher les provisions qu'ils ont cachées à l'automne.

LT ▶ The squirrels go to look for the provisions that they have hidden at the autumn.

NT ▶ Squirrels will be looking for the provisions they hid in autumn.

•••

FS ▶ Les oiseaux qui n'ont pas migré vont venir aux mangeoires installées dans les jardins.

LT ▶ The birds that have not migrated go to come to the feeders installed in the gardens.

NT ▶ Birds that haven't migrated will come to the feeders in the gardens.

•••

FS ▶ Comment la faune locale va-t-elle s'adapter à ces conditions difficiles ?

LT ▶ How the fauna local goes to itself adapt to these conditions difficult?

NT ▶ How will local wildlife adapt to these harsh conditions?

•••

FS ▶ Ces changements de saisons vont influencer non seulement notre façon de nous habiller, mais aussi le comportement des animaux et le cycle de la nature.

LT ▶ These changes of seasons go to influence not only our way of ourselves to dress, but also the behavior of the animals and the cycle of the nature.

▼

NT ▶ These seasonal changes will influence not only how we dress but also animal behavior and nature's cycle.

•••

FS ▶ Chaque saison va apporter son lot de beautés et de défis.

LT ▶ Each season goes to bring its share of beauties and of challenges.

▼

NT ▶ Each season will bring its own share of beauty and challenges.

•••

FS ▶ Il sera intéressant d'observer comment la flore et la faune vont s'adapter à ces variations climatiques.

LT ▶ It will be interesting of to observe how the flora and the fauna go itself to adapt to these climatic variations.

▼

NT ▶ It will be fascinating to see how flora and fauna adapt to these climate changes.

•••

FS ▶ N'oubliez pas de consulter régulièrement les prévisions météo pour vous préparer au mieux aux conditions à venir.

LT ▶ Forget not of to consult regularly the forecasts weather for yourself to prepare at best for the conditions to come.

▼

NT ▶ Don't forget to check the weather forecast regularly to prepare for upcoming conditions.

•••

FS ▶ Profitez bien de chaque saison !

LT ▶ Enjoy well of each season!

NT ▶ Make the most of each season!

***

Put Your Learning to the Test

1. Translate the following sentences using the vocabulary from the story:

   a) Au printemps, les températures vont augmenter progressivement.

   ____

   b) En été, les journées seront longues et le soleil brillera fortement.

   ____

   c) À l'automne, les feuilles des arbres vont changer de couleur avant de tomber.

   ____

   d) En hiver, il va neiger dans certaines régions et les températures vont descendre sous 0°C.

   ____

2. Rearrange the order of the following words to form a correct sentence:

   a) printemps au se progressivement va réchauffer temps Le

   ____

b) journées longues plus les été, En seront

___

c) feuilles tombent arbres des les vont automne, En

___

d) températures hiver, vont les baisser En fortement

___

3. Translate the following words from French to English:

a) averses ___ d) migrateurs ___

b) bourgeonner ___ e) gel ___

c) écharpe ___ f) faune ___

4. Translate the following words from English to French:

a) forecast ___ d) snowfall ___

b) season ___ e) hibernate ___

c) harvest ___ f) wind ___

5. As per the story, what should people do in winter to protect themselves from the cold?

a) Rely on central heating and avoid going outside.

b) Wear warm clothing such as coats, scarves, gloves, and hats.

c) Drink hot beverages regularly to stay warm.

d) Exercise frequently outdoors to generate body heat.

6. Complete the sentences with the correct word from the list:

Words: température, soleil, neige, parapluie

Use each word only once

a) En été, le ______________ brille et réchauffe l'atmosphère.

b) En hiver, la ______________ tombe et couvre le sol d'un manteau blanc.

c) Au printemps, la ______________ commence à augmenter lentement.

d) En automne, il pleut souvent, alors il est utile d'avoir un ______________.

7. Determine if the following statements are true or false:

a) _______ The warmest season will be spring.

b) _______ Some birds migrate south during autumn.

c) _______ During winter, temperatures in France often remain above 10°C.

d) _______ The text mentions that insects like bees and butterflies will be active in summer.

Review your answers on the next page.

Answer Key

1. a) In spring, temperatures will gradually rise.

   b) In summer, the days will be long, and the sun will shine brightly.

   c) In autumn, the leaves on the trees will change color before falling.

   d) In winter, it will snow in some regions, and temperatures will drop below 0°C.

2. a) Le temps va se réchauffer progressivement au printemps.

   b) En été, les journées seront plus longues.

   c) En automne, les feuilles des arbres vont tomber.

   d) En hiver, les températures vont baisser fortement.

3. a) showers b) bud c) scarf

   d) migratory e) frost f) wildlife

4. a) prévisions b) saison c) récolte

   d) chute de neige e) hiberner f) vent

5. b) Wear warm clothing such as coats, scarves, gloves, and hats.

6. a) soleil b) neige c) température d) parapluie

7. a) False b) True c) False d) True

Loved *Easy French Short Stories for Beginners Volume 1*? Keep progressing with Volume 2, featuring new engaging stories, essential vocabulary, and interactive exercises to help you advance your French skills.

Get Your Copy Today!

Search on Amazon for
Easy French Short Stories for Beginners Volume 2
and continue improving your French skills!

À ▶ At
Accord ▶ Agreement
Acheter ▶ To buy
Adresse ▶ Address
Aide ▶ Help
Aider ▶ To help
Aimer ▶ To love
Ainsi ▶ Thus
Air ▶ Air
Ajouter ▶ To add
Allée ▶ Path
Aller ▶ To go
Allô/Salut ▶ Hello
Alors ▶ Then
Ami/Amie ▶ Friend
Amour ▶ Love
Amusant ▶ Fun
An/Année ▶ Year
Ananas ▶ Pineapple
Animal ▶ Animal
Anniversaire ▶ Birthday
Août ▶ August
Apercevoir ▶ To perceive
Appareil ▶ Device
Appel ▶ Call
Appeler ▶ To call
Apporter ▶ To bring
Apprendre ▶ To learn
Approcher ▶ To approach
Après ▶ After
Arbre ▶ Tree
Argent ▶ Silver/Money
Arrêter ▶ To stop
Arriver ▶ To arrive
Assez ▶ Enough
Assiette ▶ Plate
Assis ▶ Seated
Attendre ▶ To wait
Attention ▶ Attention
Attraper ▶ To catch
Au-dessus ▶ Above
Au/Aux ▶ To the
Augmenter ▶ To increase
Aujourd'hui ▶ Today
Aussi ▶ Also
Aussitôt ▶ Immediately
Autant ▶ As Much
Auto ▶ Car
Autobus ▶ Bus
Automne ▶ Autumn
Autoroute ▶ Highway
Autour ▶ Around
Autre ▶ Other
Avant ▶ Before
Avantage ▶Advantage
Avec ▶ With
Avion ▶ Plane
Avoir ▶ To have
Avril ▶ April
Bagarre ▶ Fight
Bague ▶ Ring
Baignoire ▶ Bathtub
Bain ▶ Bath
Balcon ▶ Balcony
Balle/Boule ▶ Ball
Ballon ▶ Balloon
Banane ▶ Banana
Banque ▶ Bank
Barbe ▶ Beard
Bateau ▶ Boat
Battre ▶ To beat
Beau/Bel/Belle ▶ Beautiful
Beaucoup ▶ A lot
Bébé ▶ Baby
Besoin ▶ Need
Bêtise ▶ Mistake/Nonsense
Beurre ▶ Butter
Bibliothèque ▶ Library
Bicyclette ▶ Bicycle
Bien ▶ Well/Good
Bientôt ▶ Soon
Bizarre ▶ Strange
Blague ▶ Joke
Blanc/Blanche ▶ White
Blessure ▶ Injury
Bleu/Bleue ▶ Blue
Bœuf ▶ Beef
Boire ▶ To drink
Bois ▶ Wood
Boisson ▶ Drink
Boîte ▶ Box
Bol ▶ Bowl
Bon/Bonne ▶ Good
Bonbon ▶ Candy
Bonheur ▶ Happiness
Bonjour ▶ Hello
Bonsoir ▶ Good evening
Botte ▶ Boot
Bouche ▶ Mouth
Boucher ▶ Butcher

Bouger ▶ To move
Boulanger ▶ Baker
Bout ▶ End
Bouteille ▶ Bottle
Boutique ▶ Shop
Bouton ▶ Button
Branche ▶ Branch
Bras ▶ Arm
Brosse ▶ Brush
Bruit ▶ Noise
Brun ▶ Brown
Bulle ▶ Bubble
Bureau ▶ Office
Ça ▶ That
Cacher ▶ To hide
Cadeau ▶ Gift
Café ▶ Coffee
Cage ▶ Cage
Cahier ▶ Notebook
Caisse ▶ Cash register
Calme ▶ Calm
Camion ▶ Truck
Campagne ▶ Countryside
Canard ▶ Duck
Carnet ▶ Notebook
Carotte ▶ Carrot
Carré ▶ Square
Carte ▶ Card/Map
Casser ▶ To break
Cauchemar ▶ Nightmare
Ce/Cet/Cette ▶ This/That
Cela ▶ That
Celui-ci/Celle-ci ▶ This one
Celui/Celle ▶ The one
Cent ▶ One hundred
Ces ▶ These/Those
Chacun/Chacune ▶ Each one
Chagrin ▶ Sorrow
Chaise ▶ Chair
Chambre ▶ Room
Champ ▶ Field
Champignon ▶ Mushroom
Chance ▶ Luck
Chanson ▶ Song
Chanter ▶ To sing
Chapeau ▶ Hat
Chaque ▶ Each
Chat ▶ Cat
Chaton ▶ Kitten
Chaud ▶ Hot
Chauffeur ▶ Driver
Chaussure ▶ Shoe
Chemin ▶ Path
Chemise ▶ Shirt
Cher ▶ Dear/Expensive
Chercher ▶ To search
Cheval ▶ Horse
Cheveux ▶ Hair
Chez ▶ At/To (Someone's Place)
Chien ▶ Dog
Chocolat ▶ Chocolate
Choisir ▶ To choose
Choix ▶ Choice
Chose ▶ Thing
Ciel ▶ Sky
Cinéma ▶ Cinema
Cinq ▶ Five
Cinquante ▶ Fifty
Circulation ▶ Traffic
Ciseau ▶ Scissors
Citron ▶ Lemon
Classe ▶ Class
Clé ▶ Key
Cochon ▶ Pig
Cœur ▶ Heart
Coiffeur ▶ Hairdresser
Coin ▶ Corner
Colère ▶ Anger
Colle ▶ Glue
Colorier ▶ To color
Combien ▶ How much/many
Commander ▶ To order
Comme ▶ Like/As
Commencer ▶ To begin
Comment ▶ How
Compléter ▶ To complete
Comprendre ▶ To understand
Compte ▶ Account
Compter ▶ To count
Confiture ▶ Jam
Connaître ▶ To know
Connexion ▶ Connection
Conseil ▶ Advice
Construire ▶ To build
Content ▶ Happy
Continuer ▶ To continue
Contraire ▶ Opposite
Contre ▶ Against
Copain ▶ Friend/Boyfriend
Copine ▶ Friend/Girlfriend
Corps ▶ Body
Costume ▶ Suit
Côté ▶ Side
Cou ▶ Neck
Couleur ▶ Color
Coup ▶ Blow/Hit

Cuisiner ▶ To cook
Culotte ▶ Panties
Dame ▶ Lady
Danger ▶ Danger
Dans ▶ In
Danse ▶ Dance
Danser ▶ To dance
De ▶ Of/From
Debout ▶ Standing
Début ▶ Beginning
Décembre ▶ December
Décider ▶ To decide
Décision ▶ Decision
Découvrir ▶ To discover
Dedans ▶ Inside
Dehors ▶ Outside
Déjà ▶ Already
Déjeuner ▶ Lunch
Demain ▶ Tomorrow
Demande ▶ Request
Demander ▶ To ask
Dent ▶ Tooth
Dentiste ▶ Dentist
Départ ▶ Departure
Depuis ▶ Since
Dernier/Dernière ▶ Last
Derrière ▶ Behind
Dès ▶ As soon as
Des ▶ Some
Désolé ▶ Sorry
Désordre ▶ Disorder
Dessert ▶ Dessert
Dessin ▶ Drawing
Dessiner ▶ To draw
Dessus ▶ Above
Deux ▶ Two
Deuxième ▶ Second
Devant ▶ In front of
Devoir ▶ Must/Should
Difficile ▶ Difficult
Dimanche ▶ Sunday
Dîner ▶ Dinner
Dire ▶ To say
Diriger ▶ To direct
Discrètement ▶ Discreetly
Discuter ▶ To discuss
Dix ▶ Ten
Docteur ▶ Doctor
Doigt ▶ Finger
Donc ▶ Therefore
Donner ▶ To give
Dormir ▶ To sleep
Dos ▶ Back
Doucement ▶ Softly
Douche ▶ Shower
Douze ▶ Twelve
Droite ▶ Right
Drôle ▶ Funny
Du ▶ Of the
Dur ▶ Hard
Eau ▶ Water
Echelle ▶ Ladder
Ecole ▶ School
Ecouter ▶ To listen
Ecran ▶ Screen
Ecrire ▶ To write
Ecriture ▶ Writing
Eglise ▶ Church
Elève ▶ Student
Elle ▶ She
Elles ▶ They (Feminine)
Embrasser ▶ To kiss
Emporter ▶ To take away
En ▶ In/On
Encore ▶ Again
Endroit ▶ Place
Enfant ▶ Child
Enfin ▶ Finally
Ennui ▶ Boredom
Ennuyer ▶ To annoy
Enorme ▶ Enormous
Ensemble ▶ Together
Ensuite ▶ Then
Entendre ▶ To hear
Entourer ▶ To surround
Entre ▶ Between
Entrée ▶ Entrance
Entrer ▶ To enter
Envie ▶ Desire
Épaule ▶ Shoulder
Équipe ▶ Team
Escalier ▶ Stairs
Essayer ▶ To try
Essence ▶ Gasoline
Et ▶ And
Été ▶ Summer
Étoile ▶ Star
Étrange ▶ Strange
Être ▶ To be
Eux ▶ Them
Exemple ▶ Example
Exercice ▶ Exercise
Expliquer ▶ To explain
Extraordinaire ▶ Extraordinary
Fabriquer ▶ To make
Fâché ▶ Angry

Facile ▶ Easy
Facture ▶ Bill
Faible ▶ Weak
Faim ▶ Hunger
Faire ▶ To do/make
Fait ▶ Done/Made
Famille ▶ Family
Farine ▶ Flour
Faute ▶ Fault
Faux ▶ False
Femme ▶ Woman
Fenêtre ▶ Window
Fer ▶ Iron
Fête ▶ Party/Celebration
Feu ▶ Fire
Feuille ▶ Leaf
Février ▶ February
Fier ▶ Proud
Figure ▶ Face/Figure
Fille ▶ Girl
Film ▶ Movie
Fils ▶ Son
Fin ▶ End
Fini ▶ Finished
Fleur ▶ Flower
Fois ▶ Time
Fond ▶ Bottom
Forêt ▶ Forest
Forme ▶ Shape/Form
Fort ▶ Strong
Fou ▶ Crazy
Foule ▶ Crowd
Four ▶ Oven
Frais ▶ Fresh
Fraise ▶ Strawberry
Framboise ▶ Raspberry
Frère ▶ Brother
Froid ▶ Cold
Fromage ▶ Cheese
Fruit ▶ Fruit
Fumée ▶ Smoke
Fumer ▶ To smoke
Gagner ▶ To win
Garage ▶ Garage
Garçon ▶ Boy
Gardien ▶ Guardian
Gare ▶ Station
Gâteau ▶ Cake
Gauche ▶ Left
Géant ▶ Giant
Génial ▶ Great
Genou ▶ Knee
Gens ▶ People
Gentil ▶ Kind
Glace ▶ Ice cream/Ice
Glisser ▶ To slip
Gourmand ▶ Greedy
Goûter ▶ To taste
Grand ▶ Big/Tall
Grand-mère ▶ Grandmother
Grand-père ▶ Grandfather
Grandir ▶ To grow
Grignoter ▶ To nibble
Gris ▶ Gray
Gros ▶ Big/Fat
Groupe ▶ Group
Guerre ▶ War
Guide ▶ Guide
Guitare ▶ Guitar
Habiller ▶ To dress
Habit ▶ Clothes
Habiter ▶ To live
Habitude ▶ Habit
Haut ▶ High
Hélicoptère ▶ Helicopter
Herbe ▶ Grass
Heure ▶ Hour
Heureusement ▶ Fortunately
Heureux ▶ Happy
Hier ▶ Yesterday
Histoire ▶ Story
Hiver ▶ Winter
Homme ▶ Man
Hôpital ▶ Hospital
Horloge ▶ Clock
Hôtel ▶ Hotel
Huile ▶ Oil
Huit ▶ Eight
Ici ▶ Here
Idée ▶ Idea
Il ▶ He
Île ▶ Island
Ils ▶ They (Masculine)
Infirmier/Infirmière ▶ Nurse
Inquiet ▶ Worried
Installer ▶ To install
Instant ▶ Moment
Inutile ▶ Useless
Jamais ▶ Never
Jambe ▶ Leg
Jambon ▶ Ham
Janvier ▶ January
Jardin ▶ Garden
Jaune ▶ Yellow
Je ▶ I
Jeter ▶ To throw

Jeu ▶ Game
Jeudi ▶ Thursday
Jeune ▶ Young
Joie ▶ Joy
Joli/Jolie ▶ Pretty
Joue ▶ Cheek
Jouer ▶ To play
Jouet ▶ Toy
Joueur ▶ Player
Jour/Journée ▶ Day
Journal ▶ Newspaper
Joyeux ▶ Joyful
Juillet ▶ July
Juin ▶ June
Jupe ▶ Skirt
Jus ▶ Juice
Jusque/Jusqu'à ▶ Until/Up to
Juste ▶ Just/Right
Kilo ▶ Kilogram
La ▶ The (Feminine)
Là ▶ There
Là-bas ▶ Over there
Là-haut ▶ Up there
Lac ▶ Lake
Laisser ▶ To leave (Something)
Lait ▶ Milk
Lampe ▶ Lamp
Langue ▶ Tongue/Language
Lapin ▶ Rabbit
Laquelle ▶ Which one (Feminine)
Lavabo ▶ Sink
Laver ▶ To wash
Le ▶ The (Masculine)
Leçon ▶ Lesson
Léger ▶ Light (in weight)
Légume ▶ Vegetable
Lendemain ▶ Next day
Lent ▶ Slow
Lentement ▶ Slowly
Lequel ▶ Which one (Masculine)
Les ▶ The (Plural)
Lettre ▶ Letter
Leur ▶ Their
Lever ▶ To raise/lift
Libre ▶ Free
Lieu ▶ Place
Ligne ▶ Line
Limonade ▶ Lemonade
Lire ▶ To read
Liste ▶ List
Lit ▶ Bed
Litre ▶ Liter
Livre ▶ Book
Loin ▶ Far
Longtemps ▶ A long time
Lourd ▶ Heavy
Lui ▶ Him/Her
Lumière ▶ Light
Lundi ▶ Monday
Lune ▶ Moon
Lunette ▶ Glasses
Ma/Mon ▶ My
Machine ▶ Machine
Madame ▶ Madam
Magasin ▶ Store
Magique ▶ Magic
Magnifique ▶ Magnificent
Mai ▶ May
Maigre ▶ Skinny
Maillot ▶ Jersey/Swimsuit
Main ▶ Hand
Maintenant ▶ Now
Mais ▶ But
Maison ▶ House
Maître/Maîtresse ▶ Teacher/Master
Mal ▶ Bad
Malade ▶ Sick
Maman ▶ Mom
Manche ▶ Handle/Sleeve
Manger ▶ To eat
Marchand ▶ Merchant
Marché ▶ Market
Marcher ▶ To walk
Mardi ▶ Tuesday
Marron ▶ Brown
Mars ▶ March
Marteau ▶ Hammer
Masque ▶ Mask
Matelas ▶ Mattress
Matériel ▶ Material/Equipment
Matin ▶ Morning
Méchant ▶ Mean
Mélodie ▶ Melody
Même ▶ Same
Menton ▶ Chin
Menu ▶ Menu
Mer ▶ Sea
Merci ▶ Thank you
Mercredi ▶ Wednesday
Mère ▶ Mother
Mes ▶ My (Plural)
Message ▶ Message
Messieurs ▶ Gentlemen
Métier ▶ Profession/Trade
Métro ▶ Subway

Mettre ▶ To put
Meuble ▶ Furniture
Midi ▶ Noon
Miel ▶ Honey
Mien ▶ Mine
Mieux ▶ Better
Mignon ▶ Cute
Milieu ▶ Middle
Mille ▶ Thousand
Minute ▶ Minute
Miroir ▶ Mirror
Modèle ▶ Model
Moi/Me ▶ Me
Moins ▶ Less
Mois ▶ Month
Moitié ▶ Half
Moment ▶ Moment
Mon ▶ My (Masculine)
Monde ▶ World
Monsieur ▶ Mr./Gentleman
Montagne ▶ Mountain
Monter ▶ To climb
Montre ▶ Watch
Morceau ▶ Piece
Mot ▶ Word
Moteur ▶ Engine
Moto ▶ Motorcycle
Moustache ▶ Mustache
Mouton ▶ Sheep
Moyen ▶ Means/Method
Mur ▶ Wall
Musique ▶ Music
Nage ▶ Swimming
Nager ▶ To swim
Nain ▶ Dwarf
Nature ▶ Nature
Naturel ▶ Natural
Né ▶ Born
Ne ▶ Not
Nécessaire ▶ Necessary
Neige ▶ Snow
Nettoyer ▶ To clean
Neuf ▶ Nine/New
Nez ▶ Nose
Ni ▶ Neither/Nor
Noël ▶ Christmas
Noir/Noire ▶ Black
Nom ▶ Name
Nombre ▶ Number
Non ▶ No
Nos ▶ Our (Plural)
Note ▶ Note
Notre ▶ Our (Singular)
Nourriture ▶ Food
Nous ▶ We
Nouveau/Nouvelle ▶ New
Novembre ▶ November
Nuage ▶ Cloud
Nuit ▶ Night
Numéro ▶ Number
Objectif ▶ Goal
Objet ▶ Object
Observer ▶ To observe
Occupé ▶ Busy
Occuper ▶ To occupy
Océan ▶ Ocean
Octobre ▶ October
Odeur ▶ Smell
Œil ▶ Eye
Œuf ▶ Egg
Oignon ▶ Onion
Oiseau ▶ Bird
Ombre ▶ Shadow
On ▶ One/We
Oncle ▶ Uncle
Onze ▶ Eleven
Or ▶ Gold
Orage ▶ Storm
Orange ▶ Orange (Fruit/Color)
Ordinateur ▶ Computer
Ordre ▶ Order
Oreille ▶ Ear
Os ▶ Bone
Ou ▶ Or
Où ▶ Where
Oublier ▶ To forget
Oui ▶ Yes
Ouvrir ▶ To open
Page ▶ Page
Pain ▶ Bread
Paire ▶ Pair
Panier ▶ Basket
Panne ▶ Breakdown
Pantalon ▶ Pants
Papa ▶ Dad
Papier ▶ Paper
Papillon ▶ Butterfly
Paquet ▶ Package
Par ▶ By
Parapluie ▶ Umbrella
Parc ▶ Park
Pardon ▶ Sorry
Parent ▶ Parent
Parfois ▶ Sometimes
Parler ▶ To speak
Parmi ▶ Among

Part ▶ Part/Share
Partie ▶ Part
Partir ▶ To leave
Partout ▶ Everywhere
Pas ▶ Not/Step
Passer ▶ To pass
Pâte ▶ Dough/Paste
Pâtes ▶ Pasta
Pâtisserie ▶ Pastry
Pauvre ▶ Poor
Payer ▶ To pay
Pays ▶ Country
Peau ▶ Skin
Peindre ▶ To paint
Peine ▶ Pain/Sorrow
Peinture ▶ Painting
Peluche ▶ Plush toy
Pendant ▶ During/While
Pensée ▶ Thought
Penser ▶ To think
Perdre ▶ To lose
Perdu ▶ Lost
Père ▶ Father
Personne ▶ Person/Nobody
Petit/Petite ▶ Small
Peu ▶ Little/Few
Peur ▶ Fear
Peut-être ▶ Maybe
Pharmacie ▶ Pharmacy
Photo ▶ Photo
Phrase ▶ Sentence
Pièce ▶ Piece/Room
Pied ▶ Foot
Pierre ▶ Stone
Pile/Batterie ▶ Battery
Pinceau ▶ Paintbrush
Piscine ▶ Swimming pool
Placard/Armoire ▶ Cupboard
Place ▶ Square/Place
Plage ▶ Beach
Plaisir ▶ Pleasure
Planche ▶ Plank
Plante ▶ Plant
Plastique ▶ Plastic
Plat ▶ Dish
Plateau ▶ Tray
Plein/Pleine ▶ Full
Pleurer ▶ To cry
Pleuvoir ▶ To rain
Pluie ▶ Rain
Plume ▶ Feather
Plus ▶ More
Poche ▶ Pocket
Poésie ▶ Poetry
Poil ▶ Hair (Body hair)
Point ▶ Point
Poire ▶ Pear
Pois ▶ Pea
Poisson ▶ Fish
Police ▶ Police
Pomme ▶ Apple
Pomme de terre ▶ Potato
Pompier ▶ Firefighter
Pont ▶ Bridge
Portable ▶ Mobile phone/Portable
Porte ▶ Door
Porter ▶ To carry
Poser ▶ To put down
Poste ▶ Post office/Job
Poster ▶ To post
Pouce ▶ Thumb
Poule/Poulet ▶ Chicken
Pour ▶ For
Pourquoi ▶ Why
Pourtant ▶ Yet
Pousser ▶ To push
Pouvoir ▶ To be able to/can
Préférer ▶ To prefer
Premier/Première ▶ First
Prendre ▶ To take
Préparer ▶ To prepare
Près ▶ Near
Presque ▶ Almost
Prêt ▶ Ready
Printemps ▶ Spring
Privé ▶ Private
Prix ▶ Price
Produit ▶ Product
Professeur ▶ Teacher/Professor
Programme ▶ Program
Promenade ▶ Walk/Stroll
Promener ▶ To walk
Proposer ▶ To suggest
Propre ▶ Clean
Public ▶ Public
Puis ▶ Then
Pull ▶ Sweater
Pyjama ▶ Pajamas
Quand ▶ When
Quarante ▶ Forty
Quartier ▶ Neighborhood
Quatorze ▶ Fourteen
Quatre ▶ Four
Quatre-vingt-dix ▶ Ninety
Quatre-vingts ▶ Eighty
Que ▶ That/What

Quel/Quelle ▶ Which
Quelqu'un ▶ Someone
Quelque ▶ Some
Question ▶ Question
Queue ▶ Tail/Line
Qui ▶ Who
Quinze ▶ Fifteen
Quoi ▶ What
Raconter ▶ To tell
Radio ▶ Radio
Raisin ▶ Grape
Raison ▶ Reason
Ralentir ▶ To slow down
Ramasser ▶ To gather/pick up
Rang ▶ Row/Rank
Ranger ▶ To tidy up
Rapide ▶ Fast
Rapidement ▶ Quickly
Rare ▶ Rare
Ravissant ▶ Delightful
Réaliser ▶ To realize
Réalité ▶ Reality
Récemment ▶ Recently
Recevoir ▶ To receive
Réchauffer ▶ To warm up
Récit ▶ Story
Reconnaître ▶ To recognize
Reculer ▶ To step back
Refuser ▶ To refuse
Regarder ▶ To watch
Région ▶ Region
Règle ▶ Rule/Ruler
Regret ▶ Regret
Relation ▶ Relationship
Remède ▶ Remedy
Remettre ▶ To put back
Remplir ▶ To fill
Rencontre ▶ Encounter
Rencontrer ▶ To meet
Rendez-vous ▶ Appointment
Rentrer ▶ To return
Renverser ▶ To knock over
Réparer ▶ To repair
Repas ▶ Meal
Répéter ▶ To repeat
Répondre ▶ To answer
Réponse ▶ Answer
Reposer ▶ To rest
Restaurant ▶ Restaurant
Reste ▶ Rest/Remainder
Rester ▶ To stay
Résultat ▶ Result
Résumer ▶ To summarize
Retard ▶ Delay
Retenir ▶ To retain
Retour ▶ Return
Retourner ▶ To return
Retrouver ▶ To find
Réunion ▶ Meeting
Rêve ▶ Dream
Réveil ▶ Alarm clock
Réveiller ▶ To wake up
Revenir ▶ To come back
Revenu ▶ Income
Rhume ▶ Cold (Illness)
Riche ▶ Rich
Ridicule ▶ Ridiculous
Rien ▶ Nothing
Rire ▶ To laugh
Rivière ▶ River
Riz ▶ Rice
Robe ▶ Dress
Robinet ▶ Faucet
Robot ▶ Robot
Rochers ▶ Rocks
Rond ▶ Round
Rose ▶ Pink
Roue ▶ Wheel
Rouge ▶ Red
Route ▶ Road
Rue ▶ Street
Sa/Son ▶ Her/His (Feminine)
Sable ▶ Sand
Sac ▶ Bag
Sage ▶ Wise
Salade ▶ Salad
Sale ▶ Dirty
Salle ▶ Room
Salon ▶ Living room
Samedi ▶ Saturday
Sans ▶ Without
Santé ▶ Health
Sauter ▶ To jump
Savoir ▶ To know
Savon ▶ Soap
Secours ▶ Help
Secret ▶ Secret
Sécurité ▶ Security
Seize ▶ Sixteen
Sel ▶ Salt
Semaine ▶ Week
Sentir ▶ To feel/smell
Sept ▶ Seven
Septembre ▶ September
Service ▶ Service
Ses ▶ His/Her (Plural)

Seul/Seule ▶ Alone
Seulement ▶ Only
Si ▶ If
Signe ▶ Sign
Silence ▶ Silence
Singe ▶ Monkey
Sinon ▶ Otherwise
Six ▶ Six
Sœur ▶ Sister
Soif ▶ Thirst
Soigner ▶ To take care of
Soin ▶ Care
Soir ▶ Evening
Soixante ▶ Sixty
Soixante-dix ▶ Seventy
Sol ▶ Ground
Soleil ▶ Sun
Solide ▶ Solid
Sommeil ▶ Sleep
Sonner ▶ To ring
Sortir ▶ To go out
Soudain ▶ Suddenly
Souffle ▶ Breath
Soupe ▶ Soup
Sourire ▶ To smile
Sous ▶ Under
Souvent ▶ Often
Spectacle ▶ Show
Sport ▶ Sport
Station ▶ Station
Stop ▶ Stop
Stylo ▶ Pen
Sucre ▶ Sugar
Suggérer ▶ To suggest
Suite ▶ Following/Next
Suivre ▶ To follow
Sur ▶ On
Sûr ▶ Sure
Sûrement ▶ Surely
Surprise ▶ Surprise
Surtout ▶ Especially
Ta/Ton ▶ Your
Table ▶ Table
Tableau ▶ Painting/Board
Taille ▶ Size
Tant ▶ So much
Tante ▶ Aunt
Tapis ▶ Rug/Carpet
Tard ▶ Late
Tarte ▶ Pie
Tasse ▶ Cup
Téléphone ▶ Phone
Télévision ▶ Television
Tellement ▶ So much
Tempête ▶ Storm
Temps ▶ Time/Weather
Terminer ▶ To finish
Terre ▶ Earth/Ground
Tes ▶ Your (Plural)
Tête ▶ Head
Texte ▶ Text
Thé ▶ Tea
Théâtre ▶ Theater
Tirer ▶ To pull
Tiroir ▶ Drawer
Tissu ▶ Fabric
Toi ▶ You
Toilettes ▶ Toilet/Bathroom
Toit ▶ Roof
Tomate ▶ Tomato
Tomber ▶ To fall
Ton ▶ Your (Masculine)
Tôt ▶ Early
Total ▶ Total
Touche ▶ Touch/Key
Toujours ▶ Always
Tourner ▶ To turn
Tous/Toutes ▶ Everyone/All
Tout/Toute ▶ Everything/All
Tranquille ▶ Calm
Travail ▶ Work
Travailler ▶ To work
Trente ▶ Thirty
Très ▶ Very
Trésor ▶ Treasure
Triste ▶ Sad
Trois ▶ Three
Troisième ▶ Third
Trop ▶ Too much
Trottoir ▶ Sidewalk
Trou ▶ Hole
Trouver ▶ To find
Tu ▶ You
Un/Une ▶ A/One (Masculine/Feminine)
Utile ▶ Useful
Utiliser ▶ To use
Vacances ▶ Holidays
Vache ▶ Cow
Vaisselle ▶ Dishes
Valise ▶ Suitcase
Vélo ▶ Bike
Vendre ▶ To sell
Vendredi ▶ Friday
Venir ▶ To come
Vent ▶ Wind

Ventre ▶ Belly
Verbe ▶ Verb
Verre ▶ Glass
Vers ▶ Towards
Verser ▶ To pour
Vert/Verte ▶ Green
Veste ▶ Jacket
Vêtement ▶ Clothing
Viande ▶ Meat
Vie ▶ Life
Vieux ▶ Old
Village ▶ Village
Ville ▶ City
Vin ▶ Wine
Vingt ▶ Twenty
Visage ▶ Face
Visite ▶ Visit
Visiter ▶ To visit
Vite ▶ Quickly
Vitesse ▶ Speed
Voici ▶ Here is
Voilà ▶ There is
Voir ▶ To see
Voisin ▶ Neighbor
Voiture ▶ Car
Voix ▶ Voice
Voler ▶ To steal/fly
Voleur ▶ Thief
Votre ▶ Your (Formal)
Vouloir ▶ To want
Vous ▶ You (Formal/Plural)
Voyage ▶ Trip
Vrai ▶ True
Vraiment ▶ Really
Vu ▶ Seen
Y ▶ There
Yeux ▶ Eyes
Zéro ▶ Zero

Would You Like to Print This List?

You can download and print it as part of your bonus materials.

See page 12 for download instructions.

Your Feedback Matters!

Thank you for choosing *Easy French Short Stories for Beginners Volume 1*. We're excited to be a part of your French learning journey!

We'd greatly appreciate it if you could take a moment to share your experience with this book on Amazon. Your review helps others discover valuable resources and supports our mission to create tools that make language learning engaging and accessible.

How to Leave a Review:

1. Search for the book in your recent orders on Amazon or scan the QR code below.

2. A quick review, even a few words, goes a long way!

Thank you for your support and for being part of the FluentBridge Publishing community.

Happy Learning!
FluentBridge Publishing

Made in the USA
Middletown, DE
29 April 2025

74928782R00113